Prais

"Taskology delivers RESULTS. Your workday will be far more productive and much less stressful. If you haven't learned Taskology, do it now. It will change the way you work forever!"
Eddie Jenkins – CIO, Acton Mobile

"Leslie does a fantastic job of using an engaging story to portray the fast-paced life of an executive who is drowning in a sea of rapid fire emails and other communications. **Taskology** gives you a practical and efficient process to manage the tidal wave of information we all face. It is a powerful productivity system that can assist us in unplugging and taking back the time and peace that eludes so many in our business environment."
Stuart W. Welsh – Certified Business Exit Consultant® and President, EGT Advisors, LLC

"Before learning Taskology, I didn't have a system for staying on track and completing projects without having to cut into my personal time. I worked extra hours to catch up, taking time away from my family. With Taskology, I feel like I have gained more hours in my day and achieved the balance I require in my life. Thank you!"
Pat Isaac – CEO, Capital Services, Inc.

"This book hit home for me big time. Leslie Shreve reveals the reality of how being disorganized and working unproductively can impact you both personally and professionally. **Taskology** is a must-read for leaders and professionals everywhere. I highly encourage anyone who is serious about changing the way they work and reaching their goals to read **Taskology** or work with Leslie one-on-one."
Mike Mack, MBA – President, X5 Management Inc.

"I used to juggle my day by sorting through handwritten notes, email print-outs, and my CRM system. Task management and content retrieval were a sales productivity drain. Now with Taskology, I no longer wake up at night panicked that I forgot something at work. My priorities are clear, I'm working fewer hours, and I feel a sense of achievement at the end of the day."
Mary Anne Majerus-Lambert – Vice President, Advisor Sales Atlantic Division, Pax World Investments

"Prior to Taskology, my work day was much more reactive instead of proactive. I reacted to emails and issues that came up instead of consistently planning and accomplishing tasks. With Taskology, I'm more focused and purposeful. I use my time proactively to move forward instead of just trying to keep up. I feel much more satisfied and accomplished at the end of the day. I think more clearly, I'm in control of my day, and I have peace of mind."
Rob Bavar – Vice President, Bavar Properties Group, LLC

"Leslie Shreve taught me a whole new way of thinking. I can't get over how much more efficient and productive I have become. Taskology is a systematic way to approach each and every thing I do in a day."
Kate Wright – Owner and President, Wright Financial Group

"As someone who has effectively utilized the Taskology system for five years, I can attest that **Taskology** is a great book to read for those who wish to improve their productivity to rapidly become more efficient in their work and to ultimately achieve goals that previously seemed improbable."
Morris L. Garten – Fedder and Garten, PA

"Applying the lessons learned from Taskology, you'll feel more productive, more in control, more motivated, and a lot less stressed!"
Kyla O'Connell – Sales Trainer and Vice President of Business Development, ASHER

TASKOLOGY

How to Unleash the Power
of Your Most Productive Workday

LESLIE SHREVE

Published by Productive Day Publishing

Printed in the United States of America.

ISBN-13: 9780998121642
ISBN-10: 0998121649

Developmental Editor: Juli Baldwin, The Baldwin Group
Copy Editor: Brenda Quinn, The Baldwin Group
Cover Design: Melissa Cabana, Back Porch Creative
Cover Photo: Deposit Photos #11558184
Author Photo: Rich Waganer, Waganer Digital Video

Taskology® The Science of Getting Things Done and Productive Day® are trademarks of Focus Consulting, LLC.

*To my Mom and Dad, who modeled
productivity, progress and accomplishment
every day of their lives.*

Acknowledgements

FIRST AND FOREMOST, I want to thank my mother and father for their endless encouragement, enthusiasm, love and support throughout my entire life, and for helping to shape who I am today. Thank you to my dear friends, who continue to encourage me on my journey to think big, be bold, follow my dreams, and continue stretching to become the person I was meant to be. Your love and support are deeply cherished, and I am forever grateful to have you in my life.

Many thanks go to all of my clients, colleagues and customers, who inspire me to continue my mission to help leaders, professionals and corporate teams increase their efficiency, productivity, progress and achievement, and become even greater successes than they are today.

I want to thank Amy Rehkemper, who believed in me from the start, helped me spread my wings and gave me an opportunity to shine. Many thanks go to Angelique Rewers, who came up with the name of Taskology for the system I teach and for encouraging me to write this book oh-so-many years ago. Thank you to Jim Yates and Mike Hosking, who were both instrumental in providing details and true-to-life examples for the position held by the main character and the company he works for.

I want to thank Vicki Hess for introducing me to the finest editors I could have ever had the good fortune to work with. Juli Baldwin and Brenda Quinn, I couldn't have done this without you. Thank you for your patience and kindness, and for always offering sound advice and never-ending support. You helped me bring this book to life and I am grateful to you both.

Many thanks go to Melissa Cabana, who worked with me on the book cover and helped me find just the right design and layout. And thank you, Roger MacRae, for your continuous support and advice, encouragement and kindness, and high-quality work. I appreciate all you have done through the years for me and for Productive Day. I couldn't do what I do or be where I am today without you.

Table of Contents

Introduction

"...where no plan is laid,
where the disposal of time is surrendered
merely to the chance of incidence,
chaos will soon reign."

—Victor Hugo

Do you ever worry about what you missed in your email Inbox, lost on your desk, or forgot to do? Do you set out to make progress in the morning, but by the afternoon you realize you've gone in circles or jumped reactively from one interruption to the next? Maybe you feel like you're just treading water—struggling to stay afloat in the never-ending waves of information, distractions, emails, and responsibilities that only seem to grow.

If this sounds like your typical workday, you have a lot in common with the many leaders and business owners, executives and professionals, and corporate employees who experience the daily challenges of too much to do, not enough time, and too many emails.

This is how it feels for Jim Bailey, the main character of the story that follows. Jim is the regional Vice President of Sales for Octagon Office Solutions. He has enjoyed a long and successful career in sales, but now things have changed.

More specifically, Jim's workday has changed. It has become progressively busier and more chaotic, and Jim is stressed out. He doesn't know how he's going to keep up at work, much less get ahead in his career. He's in trouble with his wife for not spending enough quality time at home—in the evenings or on weekends—or on vacations. And he's on the radar of the company president, who has a watchful eye on Jim's chaos, and lately, Jim isn't earning any gold stars for his performance.

In addition, Jim's chaos is spilling over from his workday into the workdays of others—affecting other employees and causing problems for different departments at Octagon. In total, Jim is negatively affecting revenue and customer service, and he's putting the company's quality name at risk.

Jim has a choice to make. He can either continue to plod through his workdays—adding to his stress and frustration, and putting his job in danger—or he can choose to find a solution. Early on in the story, Jim contemplates how his workday became so out of control, and you may be wondering the same thing about your workday.

Like a lot of professionals, you may have been asked to do more with less in your workday, and yet meet the same annual goals. It's been a common issue since 2008 and it has worn down the corporate workforce. In 2014, the "overwhelmed employee" became an emerging trend according to Deloitte in their Global Human Capital Trends Report. As well, numerous other studies have reported increases in employee stress and burnout and their effect on productivity and progress—for both employees and the companies they work for.

Even in our own Productive Day® surveys, as of the writing of this book, almost 80% of clients, prior to engaging with Productive Day, reported feeling overwhelmed at least "sometimes," and within that group 45% felt overwhelmed "often" or "all the time." Additionally, 62% percent of new clients said they had previously used only *half* of their workday for what they intended to do. The other half of the day was lost to unproductive activities.

As a result of working this way, clients have reported feelings of guilt, anger, stress, frustration, anxiety, sadness, and overwhelm. Many have felt out of control, unfocused, drained, unsettled, nervous, inadequate and scared. Some have indicated feeling like an imposter, like a failure, or as if they weren't actually good at what they do.

Unfortunately, many professionals have resigned themselves to a workday grind that has no end... and no reprieve in sight. Many believe this kind of workday is as good as it gets. But it's not. And that's why this book was written.

If you're working with constant feelings of frustration or overwhelm, operating in a perpetual state of trying to catch up, or you never feel like you're achieving what you set out to achieve, this kind of workday is *not* as good as it gets. You *can* master your workday. You *can* increase your levels of productivity, performance and progress. You *can* reduce stress and gain more peace of mind.

And you can do all of this when you master the missing piece: workload management.

Workload management is the behind-the-scenes part of your workday. It's *how* you accomplish tasks and projects. It's *how* you manage information. It's *how* you handle your time. It's *how* you address email. It's *how* you navigate your workday and make progress.

Sure, you're smart and successful, and you have your special blend of expertise, experience, and education. But when the "how" of your workday gets in the way, these are often muted, subdued, or hidden. Your talents can be overshadowed by the chaos.

How am I going to get through all these to-dos?
How am I going to get the time I need to work on my most important priorities?
How am I going to get through all of these emails?

When your workday spins out of control, the chaos can easily overrun your expertise and put the brakes on the progress you intended to make.

In this easy-to-read business fiction—based on real client experiences—you can follow along as Jim Bailey learns a new way to manage his workday. With the help of a workload management and productivity expert named Holly Goodwin, he implements a system called Taskology® The Science of Getting Things Done.

Taskology is a proven, time-tested system that can help you banish chaos, clutter and confusion, and replace them with clarity, confidence and control. The system has been called "granular," "practical," and "atomic," and leaves no stone unturned in your workday. It's a methodology that can change the way you think about getting things done, as well as how you plan and execute.

How you work is just as important as *doing* your work, and when implemented Taskology enables you to work more efficiently and effectively—without missing, losing or forgetting anything. When you master workload management, you can achieve more of what you really want to do each day—in less time with less stress. And when you increase your levels of productivity and performance, you can make more meaningful progress, achieve more goals, and feel a greater sense of accomplishment at the end of every day.

Prepare to witness the transformation as Jim learns how to take control of his workday. But first, let's take a vacation...

CHAPTER 1

Frustration on Vacation

Jɪᴍ sᴛᴏᴏᴅ ᴀᴛ the sliding glass door and looked out at the beach. What a perfect day to be on vacation—sunny with a light breeze and not a cloud in the sky. It was 10:30 a.m. on a Monday and the beach was crowded. He was glad he'd gone out earlier this morning to stake a claim for his family in the sand close to the ocean.

What a great idea to come to the beach with Rob and Jill and their kids, he thought. His two young daughters would have friends to play with all week, and he and Julie could enjoy some downtime with their best friends. He'd been skeptical when Julie had suggested vacationing with friends, but over these first couple of days he'd realized this was the ideal vacation for everybody. He sipped his second cup of morning java and smiled as he watched his two daughters happily digging in the sand alongside Rob and Jill and their two sons. *If only I could be out there digging in the sand with them . . .*

"Are you going to join us on the beach?" said Julie as she walked by, laden with a beach bag, beach towels and a cooler.

"Honey, let me take all that stuff out to the beach for you," said Jim, setting down his coffee and his cell phone.

"Thanks, but I can manage," she said, freeing one hand to pull open the sliding glass door. She stopped and turned to him. "Make you a deal. I'll let you carry the stuff out if you agree to come out to the beach. You've been inside all morning."

Jim grinned. "Wow, that's a tempting offer." He desperately wanted to say yes, but he couldn't—not yet. Not until he was satisfied that this client issue brewing back at the office was fully resolved. Smiling at his wife, he said with hope and promise, "I can't come out quite yet. But I expect to be out there in the next half hour."

With a shake of her head and a familiar grimace, Julie opened the door and stepped onto the wooden deck. "You're on vacation, Jim!" she said over her shoulder. "Yet here you are, working. As usual . . ." her voice trailing off as she approached the stairs leading down to the beach.

"Well, at least we started out with a nice weekend . . ." Jim began, recalling two days of playing with the kids on the beach, dining on seafood and enjoying the company of good friends. That had to count for something, didn't it?

Julie stopped just before the stairs and turned to face him. "Sure, you were with us, but I know you, Jim . . . you were distracted. You were thinking about work the entire time. Is this ever going to change?" She shook her head once more as she started down the steps and headed out to the beach to join Rob and Jill and the kids.

Jim stood at the open door, wanting to say something reassuring—but what could he say that Julie hadn't heard before?

Just then, Rob got up from his beach chair and waved his arms wildly at Jim, motioning for him to come out.

A deep sense of frustration and disappointment tugged at Jim. "Yeah, rub it in, buddy," he said under his breath, but he pasted on a grin and waved back at Rob. He quickly closed the sliding glass door. "Lucky guy," he muttered, turning away. Why did Rob get to enjoy his vacation without any work crises?

Jim sat down in a living room chair and let out a deep sigh. Yes, it was a perfect summer day for relaxing on the beach—but not for him.

He wanted to deny it, but Julie had been right about the weekend—he *had* been distracted the whole time and he *had* thought about work. Sure, he'd enjoyed being on the beach and playing with the kids, but all weekend he had dreaded the arrival of Monday morning. He just knew that if it was anything like the past few vacations, Monday morning would mean urgent phone calls about one thing or another, and he'd probably have at least one crisis to solve during the week. He'd done his best to prepare for his week away, but somehow there always seemed to be something he had overlooked or forgotten to do before he'd left.

And, unfortunately, he'd been right about Monday morning. History was repeating itself.

Jim sipped his coffee and stared at his cell phone on the coffee table, willing it to ring so he could get this issue settled. He reflected on the phone call earlier this morning that had started it all. Right around 9 a.m.—just after he'd come in from staking out a spot on the beach—he'd received a call from Jennifer, his assistant at Octagon Office Solutions.

"Thought I'd better give you a heads-up," Jennifer had said, her voice tense. "We have an unhappy customer."

And why am I not surprised? Jim had thought. "OK. Fill me in."

"Remember Jack Peterson, the Purchasing Manager from Brown & Jacobs?"

"The accounting firm?" Jim felt his muscles tighten. It had taken him a year to land this high-profile new client, and the purchasing manager was already unhappy. Great. "Yeah, sure, I remember Jack. What's up?"

"Well, apparently he was expecting 18 copiers and 12 printers to be delivered and installed today—at 8 a.m. sharp, is what he said—but he just called a few minutes ago to say that the expected delivery was already an hour late, and he wanted to know what was going on. He's leaving town early this afternoon and wants to make sure the delivery is actually on its way. I'm working on it, but I thought you should know..."

Jennifer patiently explained everything she'd tried to do on her own to remedy the situation, but without the customer folder, she said, she was missing the details necessary to completely resolve the issue. Jim told her the couple of places she could look in his office to find the folder, not wanting to admit that the folder was undoubtedly buried in one of the stacks of paper and files on his desk, but he trusted that somehow Jennifer would miraculously find it.

After the phone call, he and Jennifer had exchanged text messages a couple of times as she went through his office in search of the folder. But now it was 10:30 am and nearly an hour had passed since their last communication.

Jim checked his phone yet again. He didn't like how long this was taking to resolve, but he was afraid to move until the issue was settled. "C'mon, Jen, call me. Text me," he muttered.

Jim closed his eyes and tried to relax for a moment. He'd had plenty of time to think in the last hour and a half, and gradually the details of the order were coming back to him. *I remember talking with Jack last Tuesday and he's right . . . he told me that his best date for installation was today, Monday. And I thought I sent the folder to Bob, our Logistics Manager, for scheduling. But what if I didn't?* Anxiety was gnawing in the pit of Jim's stomach and a queasy feeling came over him.

Jim tried to recall what last week had been like. Frankly, most of the week was a blur. As usual, he'd been scrambling to keep up in the midst of the constant interruptions and distractions and the steady trail of people who stopped by to ask questions. And with everything he'd been trying to wrap up before leaving on vacation, he couldn't remember much about his accounts.

He winced with a sudden realization. 'Scrambling to keep up' described pretty much every week. When had that become the norm? What had happened to him? Throughout his career he'd always prided himself on being focused, prepared and organized. These days, however, staying focused and on track was nearly impossible because of everything that happened during the day. He felt overloaded and it seemed he could never make significant progress on his projects and tasks. When he took this job he'd made a commitment to be responsive to his team, and they seemed to appreciate his open-door policy and his quick replies to emails and phone calls. But lately he realized that dropping everything to respond to his team and his colleagues came at a high price. The constant interruptions cost him time and his focus, and caused him to lose track of his priorities.

And no matter how hard he tried to keep up, he was starting to feel less prepared and less productive than ever before. He hated the disarray of papers and files that blanketed every surface in his office, but… who has time to go through all that stuff? He dealt with his colleagues' teasing jabs about his disorganization by always replying that he knew where everything was, but lately, Jim knew that wasn't true. Today's mix-up wasn't the first time that a customer's folder or paperwork had gone missing. And he shuddered at the thought of his overflowing email Inbox. He was drowning in email already, but every day at least a hundred new emails arrived and accumulated in his Inbox. Was it any wonder he could never find what he needed?

Jim silently shook his head, longing for the simplicity of his early career. Back in those days he'd been proud of his clutter-free desk, and he'd been organized, prepared and productive. But of course, that was before he was promoted into senior management. He'd worked hard to get where he was, but every promotion meant more responsibilities, busier schedules and less time. It was hard to admit, but in the past year or so Jim had gradually been feeling more and more scattered and out of control. He knew he sometimes forgot to follow up with customers, forgot to make phone calls, or forgot about next steps he had to take. And he was painfully aware that the chaos in his work life was starting to affect the company, too, causing errors in sales, delays with deliveries, problems with installations, issues with customers and, worse yet, a more sluggish revenue flow.

Just then, the sliding glass door opened, taking Jim out of his quiet turmoil.

"Daddy! I was looking for you!" Susie, his five-year-old daughter, ran over to him.

"Are you having fun playing in the sand with your sister?" He put his coffee cup down and reached out to receive her sandy hug.

"Daddy, when are you coming out to the beach? I want you to help me build a sand castle," Susie said, her face earnest.

With a smile on his face, but a heavy heart, Jim replied, "In a few minutes, honey. I'm almost finished with my work and I'll be out as soon as I can." He stood up from his chair, swept her up in a big bear hug and swung her around until she giggled.

"You go pick a good spot for your sand castle," he said, kissing her cheek and setting her down, "and I'll be out in a few minutes."

"OK, but you better come soon!" She ran out the door, leaving him with a feeling of guilt and sadness. He absolutely had to change things at work. He was robbing himself and his family of precious time together on a family vacation.

As Jim watched Susie run across the sand to join the others, his cell phone rang. The caller ID showed it was Jennifer. *Finally. Thank goodness.* "Hi, Jennifer. What did you find out?"

"Jim, it's all taken care of. After quite a bit of digging I finally found the folder in one of the piles on your desk. I talked with Bob about delivery and installation, and he called Jack to schedule it. Apparently, you told Jack you'd arrange everything for today, and while that was noted in the folder, you didn't give the folder to Bob so the delivery was never confirmed. But Jack expected the arrangements were made for this morning. Anyway, we've rescheduled it for Tuesday of next week, and while Jack wasn't too happy about the rescheduling, we're back on track with only a one-week delay."

"Thank you, Jen. Thank you so much." Jim felt a flood of relief. He'd totally hit the jackpot when he'd added Jennifer to his team. He didn't know what he would do without her.

"But there's one more thing you should know, Jim," Jennifer continued, her tone serious.

"What's that? This sounds rather ominous," Jim said.

"John got wind of this. I—"

"John?" Jim cut in. "You mean John Winfield...the owner?" Of course it was his boss, John Winfield. Who else would it be? Immediately Jim felt his anxiety start to build all over again.

"Yes, John Winfield. I was talking with Bob about it in the hallway, and didn't realize John was approaching. I guess John overheard what I said and stopped to ask questions." Jennifer paused. "Sorry, Jim, but I had to tell him everything." Jim heard the regret in her voice.

Jim closed his eyes as the dread sank in. *Terrific . . . just terrific.* In the past John had been a strong supporter, but lately it was obvious that he'd noticed the chaos in Jim's life. Just a few weeks ago John had taken him to task in a senior-level meeting over another customer issue. This latest hiccup would just make things worse, and the fallout would not be pleasant. He dreaded his next conversation with John. And now he had another thing to worry about for the rest of his vacation.

"That's OK, Jennifer," Jim said quickly. "This is my fault. It's fine. I really appreciate all your help in fixing this mess. Don't worry about John."

"OK, Jim. I'll see you next Monday," Jennifer said. "And I really hope we won't need to talk until then," she added with a laugh.

"Right! But call me if you need to," Jim said, immediately wanting to take back those words. But Jennifer had gone above and beyond to resolve this situation, and knowing this could happen again, he wanted to make himself available in case she needed him.

Jim thanked her again and ended the call. He just stood there in the middle of the living room, staring at his phone and shaking his head. How did these mix-ups keep happening? And how did they manage to happen every single time he was on vacation? Was it Murphy's Law? Or was there a real reason why things were whipping out of control?

He walked over to the sliding glass door and looked out over the beach at his family and friends. All four kids were playing in the sand, Julie and Jill were laughing, and it looked like Rob was entertaining them by acting out one of his famously outlandish stories. As Jim watched, he wondered, *how did Rob manage to leave work behind and just enjoy his vacation?* Rob was a senior executive at a commercial real estate firm, and Jim knew Rob always had a lot on his plate, but somehow he'd figured out a way to leave work behind.

At that moment Jim just wanted to be out there with them, enjoying himself. *I want my vacations back,* he thought. *I want to sit on the beach like Rob and just chill out. This is too frustrating for everyone, including me, and especially Julie.*

And he knew it wasn't just vacations that needed fixing—the problems ran much deeper. He also wanted more order and control in his workday, with less madness and unpredictability. The chaos had to stop . . . but how?

Jim was determined to find a solution. When he returned from vacation, things were going to be different. His first idea was to find out Rob's secret to work-free and worry-free vacations and decided to ask him about it during their vacation. Then he could start making changes as soon as he got back to the office.

His decision suddenly made him feel empowered. His awareness of a need for change plus his decision to take action were the start of a solution, and he immediately started to feel better. But for now, he was going to go out to the beach, try to forget about work and focus on his family. After all, he had a sand castle to build.

CHAPTER 2

Overwhelmed at the Office

"HEY, JIM. QUICK question."

Jim looked up from his desk to see Bob, the logistics manager, step into his office with a report in his hand. *Great timing, Bob,* he thought sarcastically. *It's after 5:30. Can't this wait until tomorrow?*

"What's on your mind, Bob?" Jim smiled.

"You told me you made a big sale last week to First Chesapeake Savings & Loan, but I don't see it on my weekly sales report here. Plus, I didn't get the folder. What's up?"

"Uhhh . . . I don't know," Jim replied with hesitation, trying to remember the chain of events last week.

"It's been a whole week and I should have been able to schedule the delivery and installation by now." Bob settled into a chair in front of Jim's desk. It was clear he wasn't going anywhere until he got his answer.

Jim turned to face his computer and started scrolling through his email Inbox. "I thought I had added that sale to the system after they signed the agreement," he said. *The customer agreement has to be here somewhere.* As usual he had a ton of emails, and since the signing of that agreement last week at least 500 new emails had arrived. He knew that if he didn't catch critical emails right away, they would scroll off the screen and he would easily lose track of them.

Jim felt Bob's stare bore right through him as he kept scrolling and examining emails. He knew this was a big sale, and losing track of it affected not only the installation, but also the pending revenue. He started to sweat. This wasn't the first time he'd forgotten to follow up on next steps.

Suddenly Bob got up from his chair. Impatience was etched in his face. "Well, when you figure it out, Jim, let me know. Give me the folder so I can get started on the scheduling. Have a good evening . . ." Bob's voice trailed off as he left Jim's office.

Jim sighed, feeling deflated. He was tired of losing track of tasks, emails and details. Wait a minute . . . maybe Jennifer had the folder! He called her extension and she picked up immediately.

"I don't have it, Jim. You handed me a couple folders in the last few days, but not First Chesapeake's. But I remember you made the sale, so when you find the agreement and the folder, I'm happy to update the system."

Jim hung up the phone and started digging through a few piles on his desk. Maybe the customer agreement for First Chesapeake was buried in this mess. After a few minutes, he finally found the folder under several other customer folders. The agreement was not in the folder, so he decided to conduct a *Search* in his email Inbox to find the agreement. He wished he'd thought to do a search while Bob was sitting here. Luckily, the search pulled up a batch of results and after a minute or two, he finally narrowed them down to the right email. *Eureka!* Jim thought, opening up the digitally signed agreement.

As much as he wanted to go home, he needed to get this process moving again. He carefully reviewed the agreement and the original documentation in the folder. *Good. Everything looks correct and the agreement is complete.* He'd have Jennifer update the system first thing in the morning and then he'd notify Bob. He set the folder prominently in the middle of his desk to remind him of its priority and logged off his computer. Finally he could head home.

He glanced at his watch. *Was it after 6 already?* He shook his head in frustration. He'd been back from vacation only two weeks, but it felt like six months. Actually, he felt like he'd never been on vacation at all, since he'd spent way too much of his precious vacation time solving customer crises. And of course a big stack of new issues was already waiting for him when he got back. Would he ever catch up? The emails, interruptions and phone calls never seemed to stop.

"Jim, I'm glad you're still here."

Jim's back was to the door, but he knew that voice well. He closed his eyes and quickly took a deep breath to calm his nerves, then turned his chair around to face John Winfield, the owner and president of Octagon. Jim smiled, but his stomach was doing backflips. "Hey, John . . . I was just getting ready to head out. What can I do for you?"

Jim was still treading carefully after John had grilled him about the delivery mix-up during his week of vacation, and something about John's demeanor told him this wasn't a social visit.

"What's the status of Eastern Regional Healthcare?" John said with a hint of impatience. "I thought you said it was as good as signed. What's the status?"

Jim swallowed hard, remembering he had given John that news a week or two ago. "Yes, an agreement is in the works, but you're right. I need to follow up with them again. I should be able to solidify that deal soon," Jim said as he started searching through a pile on his desk for the folder. As he shuffled through papers and files he was aware of John's disapproving stare. *Where the heck is that folder? This is ridiculous!* Jim was racking his brain trying to picture what he had done with the folder, but he just couldn't recall. He chattered on nervously as he dug through several other piles. "I think the holdup had something to do with exactly how many copier leases were up for renewal, but . . . uh, I need to check on that."

Jim turned toward his credenza and started looking through a stack of files. "I, uh . . . I was waiting for an email back from my contact there because they also wanted to add two or three new copiers to the deal, and I need to find out what they decided. She may have already sent me the email. I'm not sure. I'll have to check my Inbox again." Resigned, he gave up the search, cleared his throat and turned to face John.

John turned and shut the door to Jim's office. Jim froze. *Am I about to get fired?*

John settled into a chair. "Jim, listen. Let's just chat for a second. You're really great at what you do," he began. "You know the products inside and out. You're great with your sales team and you have solutions and ideas ready for our customers all the time. But I gotta tell ya . . . lately your attention to detail and follow-up are sorely lacking. It seems you lose focus too easily and get sidetracked, and there seem to be way too many loose ends and customer issues. Is that a fair assessment?"

Jim nodded and swallowed the lump in his throat. "Yes, that's fair. Believe me, I'm aware that a few things have slid lately."

"In fact, *quite a few* things have slid, Jim. I know you're committed," John continued. "I see the hours you spend here, but I think you could get out of here a heck of a lot earlier if you could get a handle on all of this," he said, sweeping his arm over the mess of paper on Jim's desk. "I need you to focus and stay on top of things. What's happening here is hurting our bottom line."

"I understand, John. I hear you and I'm sorry. Don't worry . . . I'm going to take care of all this," Jim said as he looked around his office. "And I'll find out the status of Eastern Regional right away. I'll check my email again, follow up tomorrow morning and give you an update as soon as I know something."

"Please do," John said curtly, raising his eyebrows as he got up from the chair.

After John left his office, Jim rubbed his temples and finally let out the breath he'd been holding. *Man...that was a close call.* He knew his lack of focus and follow up had been unnerving for John. He needed to take action right away to regain John's confidence—and his own.

Before he left for the day, he'd jot a reminder in his notebook to follow up on Eastern Regional first thing in the morning. He knew that if he didn't write it down, he'd get distracted and forget—and this was not the time to let that happen.

Jim started searching for his notebook where he kept his most recent to-dos and notes from calls and meetings. He searched his desk, sifting quickly through the piles of papers and files. When he didn't find it, he started on the piles on his credenza. *Where did that thing go?* Now he was on a new mission: he had to find that notebook. It was filled with critical information and things he had to do. After another few minutes of searching, he grabbed the nearest legal pad in frustration. He quickly scrawled a note about Eastern Regional and First Chesapeake, and set the pad next to the First Chesapeake customer folder so he'd see both in the morning.

Jim slumped back in his chair, feeling defeated. He couldn't do this anymore. He absolutely could not function in this perpetual chaos. It never used to be like this. *He* never used to be like this. He used to be full of energy and on top of his game. He used to be the go-to guy for getting things done, but he knew that wasn't the case anymore. John was right—he needed to get a handle on a lot of things. He was starting every day already feeling behind and by the end of the day he never felt satisfied that he'd had a productive day or made any progress. He was stressed out, fed up and desperate for a change.

Jim grabbed his briefcase. It was now 6:30 p.m. and he needed to get home to his family. He felt totally drained after the conversations with Bob and John, but even so he put some paperwork and a few files into his briefcase. Maybe he'd get to work on them after the kids had gone to bed.

Then Jim suddenly stopped. He could imagine how popular he'd be with Julie, arriving home at 7:00 p.m. and then working late into the evening . . . again. He could picture the disappointment on her face. He'd seen that look too many times lately, especially during their vacation when he'd had to deal with so many work calls. Their vacation . . . wait a minute. He suddenly pictured his friend Rob relaxing on the beach while he was stuck inside waiting for the phone to ring. During his vacation Jim had vowed to make a change when he returned to the office, but he'd been so busy playing catch-up that he'd forgotten to follow through with Rob. *No surprise there,* Jim thought. Just another thing that had slipped through the cracks.

Jim set down his briefcase and pulled out his cell phone. He didn't know what Rob's secret was, but it was time to find out.

Now is the time, Jim thought, scrolling through his contacts to find Rob's name. *It's time for a change.*

CHAPTER 3

Taking Action

HOLLY GOODWIN PAUSED as she entered the coffee shop and quickly scanned the area for Rob Benson, a client she'd worked with last year. Last week Rob had emailed her and asked if they could meet this morning for an informal meeting. He'd mentioned that his friend Jim was eager to meet her and learn more about her productivity consulting business.

When Holly didn't see Rob, she ordered a non-fat latte at the counter and found a seat at a quiet table in the back. She had just gotten settled when Rob entered the coffee shop and came straight over to the table.

"Rob! Great to see you again!" Holly said, smiling and extending her hand. "It was a nice surprise to get your email."

"Great to see you too! Thanks for meeting me," Rob said. "By the way, my friend Jim is on his way, but he's running behind. He texted me as I was leaving and said he got called into an emergency meeting about some customer issue. He apologized profusely and said he'll be here in a few minutes."

"That's no problem," nodded Holly, sipping her latte. "I know everyone's constantly juggling, especially on a Monday morning."

"Well, Jim Bailey is one of my best friends and he's a super guy, but based on what I've seen, I think he's constantly juggling every day of the week—and not very well," Rob said, grimacing. "I wasn't surprised to hear about the emergency meeting or the customer issue."

"Oh?" Holly said, recalling that Rob had said something similar in his email. "You mentioned that your families were at the beach together this year, but I seem to recall it wasn't quite the vacation everyone had hoped for?"

"Well, being at the beach was wonderful, and overall I think we all had a great time. But Jim ended up working quite a lot, so it wasn't as relaxing as it could have been. I felt bad for the guy. He was on his cell phone every day dealing with emails from work, or talking with various people to answer questions or resolve issues. It was really frustrating for his wife Julie, but all of us felt his stress. He wasn't relaxed, and it made the rest of us a little tense. I know Jim would have preferred to forget about work and just have fun. And poor Julie was really fed up. She said that his work interrupts *every* vacation."

"Hmm. Now I understand what you meant," said Holly, nodding.

"Jim called me a few days ago, and it sounded like he was absolutely at the end of his rope," Rob said. "He said he'd noticed how relaxed I was on vacation and asked if I could share my secret." Rob smiled. "Of course I immediately told him about Holly, my awesome productivity consultant, and how she helped me get my sanity back."

Holly grinned. "I appreciate the referral, Rob. I'm glad you reached out and contacted me. I'd be happy to help Jim."

"You know, I actually told Jim about you a year ago, shortly after I'd finished working with you. But Jim said he didn't remember even having that conversation. And he didn't remember the email I sent him with your information, either. Said he must have lost track of the email!" Rob threw up his hands. "I guess I shouldn't be surprised. So I thought I'd set up this meeting personally to make sure he connected with you this time."

"Wow. A year ago. I'm glad you followed up with him and set up this meeting. I'll see what I can do to help."

"I know you can help," said Rob, flashing a wide smile. "I'm proof of that! My work life is finally under control, thanks to you, and I'm always singing your praises. Did I mention in my email that I got a promotion a couple of months ago?"

"No, you didn't! Congratulations! That's wonderful."

Rob nodded. "Yeah, commercial real estate is definitely what I'm meant to do, but I sure felt overwhelmed for a while. Do you remember how stressed out I was when we first started working together?"

"I do remember, and believe me, I hear that a lot," said Holly. "I've worked with a lot of professionals in a lot of industries, and just about everyone says the same thing: they're stressed out, frustrated and overwhelmed – no matter how successful they are – and their workdays are often chaotic and out of control."

"Yep, that about sums it up—chaotic and out of control," Rob said, shaking his head. "I'm so glad that's not me anymore. I can't believe how much more productive my days are now. After you taught me how to get a handle on my tasks and my email, and get more time for myself, it was amazing—I really did get more clarity, confidence and control back in my workday, just like you said. I get so much more accomplished now—in less time with less stress—and as a result I've made incredible progress at work. The difference is like night and day. My wife, Jill, has noticed the change too."

"That's great news, Rob," said Holly. "And believe me, the struggles you were facing are common. All of the clients I work with have similar workday challenges: too much to do, not enough time, too many emails, and no systematic way to manage the daily onslaught of information."

Rob nodded. "Sounds familiar. And now that you've helped me become more productive and stress-free, I know you can help Jim do the same." Rob looked over as the coffee shop door swung open. "And speaking of Jim, here he is now."

Rob stood up as Jim entered. Jim waved to acknowledge him and headed to the counter to order some coffee. A few minutes later he made his way over to their table. Rob made introductions and the three of them talked for a few minutes.

"Well, with you two finally together in the same room, I believe my work here is done," said Rob, standing up. "I'll leave you two to chat and I'll head to my meeting." Then Rob said his good-byes and headed out.

"So, Jim, tell me more about what's going on at work," Holly began. "Rob tells me you're at the end of your rope."

Jim explained to Holly that he'd been with Octagon Office Solutions for almost three years. He'd started in the company as a local Sales Director and was then promoted to V.P. of Sales for the Mid-Atlantic Region about 18 months ago. He currently managed a team of sales directors, with a total of 16 direct reports.

"I love what I do, I value my team, and I'm very grateful for my assistant, Jennifer. She's very sharp, and I really don't know what I'd do without her." Jim paused. "But lately my days have been so chaotic and out of control. It seems I'm always reacting and playing catch-up. I'm tired of forgetting tasks, follow-ups and phone calls, and I hate how disorganized I feel. My office is a disaster... and my email Inbox is like a raging river—overflowing, out of control and almost certain to drown me if something doesn't change. I'm losing way too much time looking for files, emails, attachments . . ." He threw up his hands, then let them fall back on the table and slumped back in his chair.

Holly was sympathetic, and she'd certainly heard this many times before. She could tell that Jim was suffering from a lack of systems and processes to support him, which caused disorganization, reactivity and chaos—all road blocks to his productivity and progress. He was losing time he'd never get back, and the challenges of workload management were costing him—and his company—far too much. He was clearly overwhelmed and unsure of how to fix the situation, catch up, and make meaningful progress.

Jim explained that his frustrations made him feel even more stress because of the constant worry that he might drop the ball or appear incompetent to his team or his boss.

"My whole desk is covered, end to end, with papers, folders, pads, magazines, brochures—you name it." Jim shook his head in exasperation. "Half the time I can't find anything, and when I *do* find what I need it's usually at the last second – or past when I should have taken action!"

"And what about electronic documents? Do you accumulate as many of those in your computer as you do the papers on your desk?"

"Well, I save documents on my computer desktop mostly, but it's disorganized and I get frustrated looking for things. I don't look for documents in my hard drive very often, because I'm not sure where things go when I save them and I know I'd be looking for a while."

"And how many times are you getting interrupted during the day?" Holly asked.

"Too many," Jim said. "I feel like the interruptions never stop. All I hear is *Gotta minute? Gotta minute? Gotta minute?* And that's because I have to be available to my team, my colleagues, my boss, my assistant . . ." He let out a deep sigh. "As a V.P., I've got to be there for everyone, but that means I can't get any time to myself to get anything done."

Holly nodded slowly, sensing his rising frustration. "And how do you keep track of things you need to do?"

"Well, I try to stick with one spiral notebook for keeping track of to-dos, voice mails, notes from calls and meetings . . . but then I misplace it and have to start a new list somewhere else—usually on a legal pad. I have lots of legal pads on my desk, too," Jim laughed sheepishly.

Holly smiled, sympathetic. She'd seen many collections of legal pads and spiral notebooks over the years. "OK, do you use anything else to keep track of things to do?"

"Oh, yeah, I use anything I can find," said Jim. "Calendars, planners, email, post-it notes," he began, counting off the items on his fingers, "and of course my failing memory... and I use what's sitting on my desk to remind me, too, like customer folders." Holly had heard this scenario many times before.

Jim continued, "Yeah, I use all of those . . . but none of them really help me keep up. I'll cross to-dos off of my list, but after a couple of days the list is so confusing I can't tell what's left that I still have to do. I might miss something completely because of the scribbles all over the page and it's almost impossible to read."

Holly nodded. "Have you missed follow-ups?"

"Yes."

"Deadlines?"

"Yes. And I'm embarrassed when I have to say *I'm sorry*. You know, *I'm sorry I didn't call you back, I'm sorry I didn't email you, I'm sorry I couldn't find the folder, I'm sorry I was late for the meeting*," he paused and gave her a look of exasperation. "It's a never-ending stream of disappointment—for me, for my colleagues, for my account execs . . . for everybody! It's awful. And I know John has had it with me, too."

"John? Is that your boss?" Holly asked.

"Yeah, John is the company president. John has been really patient with me, but in the past year, he's been more vocal about where I can improve." Jim described a tense meeting with John the previous week and admitted how incompetent he'd felt when his boss saw that he'd lost track of some customer issues and potential deals. "During that meeting I could really see how frustrated he's become with me. He said I lack focus and I miss too many things." Jim shook his head. "That really stung, but he was absolutely right."

Jim shared with Holly his many attempts to get organized and take back control of his day. Even though he'd tried to keep everything straight, he'd often get side-tracked and react to the chaos around him. What followed was a back-slide into the chaos he was trying so hard to avoid.

"And I understand from Rob you were working during vacation, too. Is that right?" Holly asked.

"Yeah, my wife is never happy when work invades our family time." Jim leaned back in his chair and shook his head. "I can't enjoy my time away from the office because I know someone at the office will call me or email me—and it's usually because I forgot to do something before I left or a question needs to be answered or a crisis needs to be resolved. And then when I get back from a vacation, it takes *forever* to catch up." Leaning forward again, he admitted, "Actually, I feel like I never really catch up. It's like a *normal* I'm used to, but it's not optimal."

Holly chuckled softly at Jim's air quotes on the word *normal*. She understood exactly what he meant. "How many emails do you have in your email Inbox right now, Jim? Do you remember . . . approximately?"

Jim took a minute to think. "I'm embarrassed to say that I don't really know," he finally answered. "Last time I looked, I think it was around 5,000. I know it's up there somewhere."

Holly nodded silently, not at all surprised. Most of her clients had trouble keeping up with their email from day to day. At least fifty percent of her clients had between 500 and 10,000 emails in their Inboxes when she started working with them. Jim was part of the 20 percent who had 5,000 or more, but over the years Holly had seen it all—even up to 50,000 emails or more in a client's Inbox.

"But that doesn't include what I have in my email folders . . . the ones on the left side of the screen," Jim added.

"Oh, I suspected," Holly smiled, knowing that most people use a lot of email folders to store emails, too. "Do you ever lose track of things you need to do in your email Inbox?"

"Oh yeah… emails scroll off the screen and even though I flag them for follow-up, I don't always get back to them," Jim said. "And if I *do* remember to follow up, it's not always in a timely manner. But that's what it's like for everyone, right?"

"Not necessarily, Jim," Holly said gently. "The situation you're describing is not as good as it gets. You can get your Inbox to zero and learn how to keep it that way so you can really stay on top of everything and be on top of your game."

Jim's eyebrows shot up and Holly could see he was truly surprised. "Really? Zero emails in my Inbox? I didn't think that was even possible."

"I assure you—it's possible," Holly smiled. "When you use a solid task management system and learn how to process all of your emails out of the Inbox, you can truly increase your productivity without missing, losing or forgetting anything, like follow-ups, deadlines, information, opportunities, or anything else."

Jim shook his head. "Wow. I love the idea of zero in the Inbox, but I'm not sure I can actually get there."

Holly assured him that he could, then asked, "Tell me, Jim . . . what do you think your current situation is costing you?"

"My sanity," Jim shot back with a laugh.

"OK, peace of mind would be nice to have. What else? Have you missed any opportunities?"

"Oh, I know I have." Jim looked up in thought. "Let's see . . . well, I make quite a few big sales, but sometimes—no, I need to be honest here—*quite a few times* the installations were delayed because the paperwork was incomplete or I didn't hand off the customer folder or I didn't update the system with necessary details. And those delays meant other processes were delayed too. Some opportunities were delayed because I lost my notes or my to-do list, or even the entire folder, and I didn't follow up with a customer. Or I missed an email in my Inbox that required action . . ." He paused and seemed to gather his thoughts. "Let's just say that any delay in the sales process means delayed deliveries and installations and then delayed payments, too."

"OK, so you're slowing down the flow of revenue. What's that costing the company? What's the value of an average sale or leasing opportunity?" Holly asked.

Jim paused to think for a moment. "Well, of course it depends on the quantity and the type of equipment . . . but if we're talking copiers I'd say anywhere from $50,000 to $150,000 per deal."

"And how often do you think a delay is happening? Once a year? Once a quarter? Once a month?"

"Oh, at this point I'd say about once a month." He stopped suddenly. "Holy cow!" he said after a moment. "I just realized that could be worth a million dollars a year!"

Holly nodded. She'd done the calculation in her head too. Then she switched gears and asked, "Tell me, Jim, what are you most tired of in your workday?"

Jim leaned back in his chair and crossed his arms. After a few moments of contemplation he said, "I'm tired of spending time looking for things in my email Inbox, on my desk and in my office."

"OK, what else?" Holly asked, digging a little deeper.

"I'm tired of not knowing what I'm doing from day to day. My days are so unpredictable, and I end up reacting to what's going on around me instead of focusing on my priorities. I'm tired of the interruptions and being pulled in so many directions."

"And when you're interrupted and pulled in different directions, how does that make you feel?"

"Frustrated . . . scared that I'll miss something—like I usually do."

"What else do you feel?"

"This is sort of like a productivity therapy session, isn't it?" Jim said, smiling. "What else do I feel? Uh, tired. Tired and . . . over-worked . . . overwhelmed . . . over-committed." He chuckled softly. "I guess you could say I'm 'over' everything!"

Then Jim leaned forward, crossed his arms on the table and spoke in a hushed tone, as if he was admitting a dark secret. "Sometimes . . . I feel like an imposter. Seriously. Like I shouldn't be a Regional V.P. of Sales because I'm forgetting things and missing things and running around chasing my tail half the time. I feel like I'm the chief of chaos."

Holly nodded and leaned in, listening intently as Jim shared his fears. Many of her clients had admitted similar feelings. Jim seemed to sense he had a sympathetic ear, so he continued.

"And then sometimes I feel a little . . . defeated." he continued. "Deflated . . . like I want to give up, but really I don't!" Jim leaned back in his chair with an exhausted look. "I love my job and I really want to fix this."

"And we can," Holly said quickly, smiling broadly to reassure him. "I promise you we can."

CHAPTER 4

A New Beginning

As JIM TALKED with Holly in the coffee shop, he felt relieved and reassured that he'd found the right solution for the chaos in his work life. He sensed he was in good hands with Holly, judging by the questions she asked, and he understood now why Rob had recommended her. He soon felt himself relaxing and was curious to know more.

"So tell me, Holly, how did you get started doing this, and how long have you been in business? Rob told me a little bit about you, but I want to hear more. How does the consulting work?"

Holly described how she'd worked in the corporate world for more than thirteen years before establishing Productive Day in 2003. She explained how she got started, what she had discovered along the way, and what she had created since the beginning.

"I work with business owners and leaders, executives and professionals who are motivated and driven by their goals. They're inspired and care about the work they do. My clients are all over the country and when we work together, we connect on the phone and use a computer interface. Sometimes, if my clients are local, like you are, I may visit onsite for one of the appointments."

"How does this work?" Jim asked. "Do you observe people in their workday and recommend more efficient ways of doing things?"

"I don't observe my clients as they work, but I do learn a lot about them and their jobs as we work together. What I teach is a system I developed called *Taskology® The Science of Getting Things Done*. It's made up of five different components. The three leading components are task management, time management, and email management. The two supporting components include electronic document management, and paper and file management. After many years of working with clients I realized I had a repeatable system — one that's simple, logical and easy to use. I've taught it for more than a dozen years, and I continue to teach it to individuals and teams who want to master their workday and make more meaningful, powerful progress. My work with clients involves putting the system into place so they can get immediate results."

"Wow, that's great. I like the name—Taskology," Jim said, nodding with interest.

"Thanks! Yes, Taskology was a good fit because task management is the heartbeat of your workday, and it's also the heartbeat of the system. Mastering task management is key when you want to be more productive. You need to be one hundred percent aware of what you're responsible for and you need to know which priorities to pursue first. Another important part of your workday to master is email, which contains a lot of to-dos and other important information. Too many professionals use their Inbox as a file cabinet and a to-do list, but they really shouldn't. It's not an appropriate system for tracking and prioritizing tasks or for saving reference information, but when used for these purposes, it will surely sabotage your productivity."

"I hate to admit it, but I use the Inbox that way, too," Jim said slowly. "I don't know what else to do, except flag emails when I want to read or reply to them later."

"Well, we don't use flags in Taskology, but I'll show you how to integrate the to-dos coming from email with all of your other tasks, and I'll help you get your Inbox down to zero."

"You mentioned that earlier. Zero, huh . . . ?" Jim said, shaking his head in disbelief. "I don't even know what I'd do if I reached zero in my Inbox."

"Also, having an empty Inbox is not just about seeing the white space or showing it off to your colleagues . . . although those are definitely a few of the perks," Holly said with a wink and a smile. "But it's important you get to zero because it means, without a doubt, that you've seen every email, made a decision on each of them, and moved them all to a better location of either reference or action—or they're gone, meaning you've archived or deleted them. My clients love achieving this milestone and once they get to zero, they never want to let their Inbox build up ever again."

"Wow," Jim said. "An empty Inbox sounds too good to be true. That would be wonderful. I don't know the last time my Inbox was empty. Probably the first day I joined the company!"

"Well, you can get there again. We'll set up your new Taskology Task List first and then you'll use it like it's *Mission Control*. You'll have everything you need to do, want to do and dream of doing all in one place. Not all in one *day*, but all in one *system*. And later, we'll incorporate email into the Task List, where you can prioritize all of your tasks together. Do you use Microsoft Outlook® at work?"

"Yes, we do," Jim replied.

"Excellent! Then you already have the most valuable tool you'll need. I designed Taskology with Outlook in mind, although I've taught Taskology with many other systems. But Outlook, in my opinion, is the most powerful tool out there. It's a complete system with modules that integrate with one another, which is *so* important when it comes to managing tasks, time and email. And when you use the Taskology Task List to stay on top of your game, you'll know *exactly* what your priorities are from moment to moment. Nothing will slip through the cracks and nothing will get missed."

"What about all the stuff besides email?" Jim asked. "I've got a lot of paper and files stacked up everywhere in my office, and I don't know what to do with it all," Jim said, shrugging his shoulders. Just thinking about the mess in his office brought back the stress.

"Don't worry, Jim, I'll show you how to manage everything and where it will go. Plus, I also teach decision making, so as you learn Taskology you'll learn how to quickly and easily make decisions about everything you receive or bring into your workday and how to manage it. We'll cover it all—papers, files, post-it notes, attachments from emails, notes from meetings—*everything*."

"This is sounding better all the time," Jim said. "How many appointments does it take to learn everything?"

Holly proceeded to describe the flow of the consulting: they'd start with building the Task List and then talk about time management. Then they'd organize any remaining physical papers and files, and then move into the organization of all electronic documents. At the end they would get into email folder management and finally, get his Inbox to zero.

"Throughout the entire process, Jim, you'll *learn by doing,* and beginning with the first appointment you'll work the new system and get lots of practice and accountability from week to week."

"Your system sounds like it includes everything I need," Jim nodded. "So what's the next step?"

"First, let's clarify a few things. If you're *really* ready to take charge of your workday and take your productivity and performance to the next level, I need to know one thing. Are you ready to part with your spiral notebooks, legal pads and post-it notes for tracking the things you need to do? Are you ready to start using a digital list for tracking to-dos?

"Frankly, Holly, that sounds awesome," Jim said. "Paper is obviously not working for me. I'm not familiar with the Task List in Outlook, but I'm certainly open to learning a new method of using it. I can't keep doing what I'm doing. I'm tired of losing track of stuff, and I hate it when I don't have a ready answer for John and others in the company."

"I'll bet," Holly said. "We can surely fix that, but it will take some time together. Are you ready to invest some time in learning how to improve your workload management and productivity?

"Yes, absolutely," Jim said immediately. "I know you can't wave your magic wand to instantly transform my office and my workday."

"Exactly. It took some time for your workday to become what it is, and it will take some time to change it."

Holly explained that learning the Taskology system would require time and a full commitment. "When you're committed, excited and engaged, you're more likely to be successful with Taskology, not only now but also throughout your entire career. Are you ready to dive in, Jim?"

"Yes!" he said quickly. "I've got to make a change. I'm tired of being controlled by email and interruptions, and tired of always scrambling to catch up. I need more time for me. And at the end of the day, I want to go home and spend time with Julie and the kids and just *know* my day was productive."

Jim asked Holly to help him choose the consulting package that was right for him, and after they discussed options and details, Jim made his selection. Holly described the next steps, and said her assistant would be in touch to take care of the rest.

"This is going to be great," Jim said, feeling excited and relieved as they rose from the table and got ready to leave. "I'm going to get my workday back on track and take control of everything that's spinning *out* of control right now. Thank you, Holly," he said, extending his hand. "It was so great to meet you. I can't wait to get started."

CHAPTER 5

Getting Clarity

IT WAS THURSDAY morning, and Jim eagerly anticipated Holly's arrival at 9 o'clock for their first appointment. Ever since their meeting in the coffee shop, he'd been looking forward to this day and to the changes that would finally help him take control of his workday.

Jim was thinking about all the ways he'd tried to take control in the past. He had tried different kinds of notebooks and planners to keep track of things to do. He had tried time management systems and software—even a few special apps on his phone to help him keep his focus. He tried software add-ons to help with his email. But nothing worked or lasted for long. And this morning, keenly aware that Holly was due to arrive at any minute, he was embarrassed that his chaos would be on full display. He made another attempt to reduce the stacks of paper and files, but he was doing little more than shuffling them—again.

The receptionist announced Holly's arrival, and Jim went to the lobby to greet her. They chatted as he escorted her to his office.

"Please, have a seat," he said, then realized that both guest chairs still held a few papers and files. "Uh, let me get those things out of your way," he said quickly, scooping them up and putting them on the credenza. "As you can see, it's a good thing you're here."

"No worries," smiled Holly as she sat down in the empty chair and set her coffee on a coaster on his desk.

Jim sat down behind his desk and let out a big sigh. "OK, where do we start?"

"In the beginning," said Holly with a smile, "we start with the Task List. If you remember our conversation in the coffee shop, I told you about the five elements of the Taskology system. The most important part is task management, because it's about getting things done."

Jim nodded. "I do remember, and I could really use better way to get things done."

"I hear that a lot," smiled Holly. "By the end of today's set of lessons, you'll have a brand new Task List showing all the things you need to do all in one system. All tasks will feed into this list—no matter where they came from and no matter when you plan to take action. The Task List will give you a wonderful bird's-eye view of what you need to do and when. It'll be the driver of your workday and it will allow you to easily prioritize with confidence, which will ultimately make you far more productive with your time."

"I like the sound of putting all my tasks in one place," Jim replied, feeling relieved already. "I'm ready!"

"First," Holly began, "I'll share with you a few lessons and basic concepts of Taskology Task Management and give you the *show-and-tell* in Outlook. After that, we'll start building your new Task List,"

Holly sat next to Jim in front of his computer and she could see Outlook was already open on his screen. Holly instructed him to click on the task icon at the bottom left corner of his screen to reach the task section of Outlook. She explained that while there are two types of lists available, Taskology was designed to use the *Task List* and not the *To-Do List,* which was connected to the use of the email flag.

"Jim, I want to start by explaining the difference between project management and task management," Holly began. "One of the things I see most often is the use of a list like this for *projects* instead of *tasks*. That kind of list doesn't serve you, because you only get a list of big things you want to do, but no plan for getting them done. Seeing a list of projects with due dates doesn't help you understand when you'll *do* anything. There's no connection to time outside of the occasional deadline. When you look at a list of projects that are big, it can actually cause you to hesitate or procrastinate. So, in Taskology you'll be focused on *tasks*—teeny-tiny action steps. And when you take care of planning and executing tasks, your projects will take care of themselves."

Jim nodded. "Makes sense."

Holly continued, "Most email programs have the potential to be used for *project* management or *task* management, which can be confusing without a system to follow. Today I'm going to show you how to use the Taskology Task List to manage *tasks*, not *projects*."

"Hang on a sec, Holly," said Jim. "I understand the difference between tasks and projects, but I do like to see a list of all my projects so I know what I'm working toward. Is there a place to show all my projects?"

"In Taskology, you'll build a list of tasks, which are the small action steps that support the progress of each of your projects," Holly answered. "However, you can include the name of your project before you state your task. I'll show you what I mean when we start building the list. I think it will accommodate what you're looking for."

"OK," Jim replied. "I'll wait and see what you're talking about."

"Now, there are two important questions to ask when you're planning tasks: *what am I going to do?* and *when am I going to do it?* And I don't know about you, but I've never seen a to-do list on paper that has both of these elements—usually, it's just the *what*. Sometimes people will note *due dates* or *deadlines* for certain things that have final deadlines, but generally there's no mention of *when* they'll actually *do* a task or take next steps."

Jim nodded. "That's true. When I write out my to-do list every morning, I'm just getting things out of my head, but I don't really think about when I'm going to do it all. I just figure I'll try to do everything today. For anything that's really important, I usually just put a star next to it to remind myself that it's a priority I definitely need to work on that day."

"But, as you've probably discovered, it's unrealistic to expect you'll get everything done today," Holly said. "Even more importantly, when the list is on

Taskology Tip #1

The two most important questions to ask when planning tasks:

What am I going to do?
When am I g~~~~ ~~ ~

paper you have no ability to prioritize your tasks or have them appear in priority order, and that's exactly what we're going to change today."

Holly asked Jim to open up a new task box and continued, "There are several fields provided here, as you can see, but we're going to focus only on the fields that represent the *what* and the *when* of your task."

She pointed to the Subject field in the task box. "When people see *Subject,* they're tempted to enter a project, but instead we're going to enter a task, which will be a *small action step.* We'll change the column heading, too, so it reads `Task` and not `Subject` and that will make it easier to remember to enter a small action step. When you type your task, always use a VERB in the beginning to describe your action step. This is very important because a verb promotes *action* and using it means you're articulating *exactly* what you'll do *first* or *next.* When you start with a verb, you're identifying a task —an *action step* —and not a project."

Jim listened intently. "Is this where I can identify the customer or the project first, like you mentioned earlier, and *then* add my task?"

"Yes, that's exactly what I meant," agreed Holly. "You can put the name of your project first, then follow with a colon or a dash, and then state your task starting with a verb. You can use verbs like *call, create, review, revise, consider, send, email, research, etc...*"

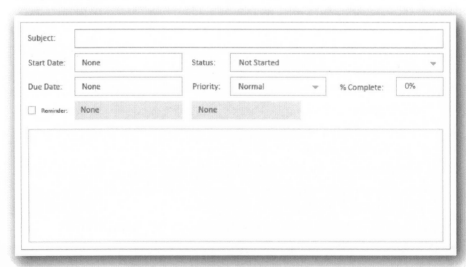

The New Task Box

Jim nodded. "Got it. Use a verb that tells me exactly what I need to do."

"Right," Holly continued. "I also want you to add all of the details about the task that you want to remember. Usually, I say *less is more* for just about everything, but when it comes to task descriptions, *more is more*. What I mean is that the more descriptive you can be about your task, the less risk you take of forgetting details and the more likely you are to dive in and take action when the time comes."

"Sounds good," Jim said. "The more details I can remember, the better off I'll be."

"So that takes care of the *what*," Holly continued. "Next, I want to explain the *when*. There are two fields available in this task box for dates—*Start Date* and *Due Date*—but if you used both of these fields, you'd stay stuck in project management thinking, which is not what you want. We're focused only on *task management* and because of that, you'll only focus on when you plan to *do* something, not when it's *due*. So for your *Do Dates,* you'll use the *Due Date* field. It's easy to remember, because *due* and *do* sound the same, but we're going to change that column heading, too, so it reads *Do Date*."

"OK, so in the *Due Date* field I'll put the date when I plan to *do* something?" Jim asked.

"Yes," Holly confirmed. "These dates are your first level of priority in Taskology. The date you choose tells you that something you plan to do today is more important or urgent to do than the task you planned for next week. It's a matter of timing. Then there's also a second level of priority that will allow you to give a meaning or a value to your tasks, which helps you prioritize *within* a day, but we'll get to that after you've built some of your Task List."

"Sounds pretty simple," Jim said. "That makes a lot of sense. And what about these other fields? There are quite a few bells and whistles in here, aren't there?" Jim remarked.

"Yes, quite a few," Holly agreed, "but you can ignore them. That's why I created Taskology—to simplify and demystify task management so managing tasks would be easier."

"What about this field called *Priority?*" Jim asked. "Isn't that kind of important?"

"Well, *priorities* are important, yes, but without a methodology to go with the technology, these bells and whistles don't always work well. I've never seen anyone use this feature successfully or with any consistency, so I created a more effective way to manage priorities in Taskology. I'll show you how to do that once you have several tasks on your Task List. That will be the *second* level of priority. And what's your first level of priority…?"

"Oh, is this a pop quiz?" Jim asked. "Uh, the first level of priority is the *Do Date*. The date I plan to do my task." He felt confident he'd given Holly the right answer, but still glanced at her for confirmation.

"Excellent! That's right," Holly said. "And the other two fields are *Status* and *Percent Complete,* which are very project-oriented, but they would be overkill for managing tasks, so you won't use those fields either. OK?"

"OK. How about this section?" Jim asked as he pointed to the screen.

"That's the *Notes* section," Holly continued. "That's where you can put additional information about a task, but *not the task itself,*" she said emphatically. "Always enter your task in the *Subject* field with the verb and all the details you can fit before using the Notes section for additional information that won't fit into the *Subject* field."

"Can you give me an example?" Jim asked.

"Sure. Let's say you create a task to email your assistant and you ask her to print three different sales reports for you. You'll have plenty of room in the *Subject* field to state your task, including the names of the three sales reports. So your task will read: *E-mail Jennifer to request sales reports…* and then you can add the names of the three sales reports on the same line. What you *don't* want to do is type *E-mail Jennifer* in the *Subject* field and then put the rest of the task in the *Notes* section. If you do, then you'll spend time double-clicking to open up the Task to see what you *really* needed to do. I know it doesn't seem like a big deal now, but when you have 20, 40 or 60 tasks to manage, you don't want to waste time double-clicking into each task, because that time adds up.

"Instead," Holly continued, "maximize your *Subject* field by typing all of the task details there. Seeing your task details right away and not hiding them will allow you to take action faster. And more importantly, when you need to reprioritize your tasks, you'll be able to do so very quickly because you can see all of your tasks—including details and *Do Dates*—all at once. We'll get to the topic of reprioritizing soon."

"OK, got it. So I'll only use the Notes section if I have to… and only after I've maximized the *Subject* field," Jim said.

"Exactly," Holly confirmed with a smile. She closed the Task box. "Now let's talk about how to view and use the main Task List screen. No matter what version of Outlook you're using, it's important to always use the view called *Simple List*." She pointed to the words on his screen. "This view allows you to access the feature at the top of the list that says *Click here to add a new Task,* which allows you to quickly and efficiently add a new task without opening the Task box every time.

"Next, we're going to rearrange the columns on your main Task List screen. The default screen for *Simple list* isn't best for Taskology Task Management, since the *Due Date* column originally appears on the right. Ideally, you want the Due Date column—holding your *Do Dates*—on the left side of the screen so you can focus first on *when* you plan to do your tasks." Holly told Jim how to rearrange the columns and moved the *Due Date* column just to the left of the *Subject* column.

"Now this is a better arrangement so you can see your action dates first and then your tasks," Holly continued. "From left to right, you now have columns for the Tasks icon, then *Attachment, Check Box, Due Date* and *Subject*. She then narrowed the *Due Date* column to the just the width of a typical date. "You want as much room as possible for your *Subject* field, since that's where you'll enter your task and all of its details. And one final thing—you won't need this *Check Box* column and I'll tell you why."

"OK," said Jim, "because I'd want to check off my tasks as I do them, like I do on my paper list, so I can see what I've completed during the day. But it sounds like that's not what I'll be doing," he finished with a chuckle.

Holly smiled in understanding. "No, you won't. If you mark tasks as *Complete* they'll show a line crossed through them, but they'll stay on your list with all of your other active tasks, unless we filter them off. But in Taskology, when you're completely finished with a task – with *no* further action steps – you'll just delete it."

"So I can't check them off and keep them somewhere else?" Jim asked.

"Well, it's not beneficial to hold onto completed tasks. They'll just build up in your system and you're not likely to ever look at them again. Is there a specific reason why you'd want to save completed tasks? Would anyone else ask for a record of those? Would you need to see them later on?"

Jim pondered Holly's questions. Finally he said, "Well... no, I guess I really don't need to keep them."

"Only if you're trying to prove something or show someone else how much you accomplished in a week," Holly said. "Most of my clients decide not to save completed tasks, but it depends on their position in the company. Since you're a leader, I don't think you need to accumulate completed tasks or spend your precious time looking at them. What do you think?"

"No, you're right," Jim said quickly. "That wouldn't make sense for me. I like the idea of checking things off my list, but I can see how all of those completed tasks could build up. I'll just delete them."

"You'll see how this works as you build and manage your list," said Holly. "Many tasks will have follow-up steps, so you won't delete them right away. Instead, you'll change them to reflect the *next* action step and you'll change the *Do Date*. They'll stay on your list until you take action again, but when you've *truly* completed the very last action step, then you can delete the task."

"Can you give me an example?" Jim asked.

"Sure. Let's say you call a prospect today—her name is Jane—and you speak with Jane about a brand new line of copiers on the market. You've already shown her a few options, but this series is brand new, and she agrees to take a look. So when you get off the phone, you adjust your original task to capture your *next* action step. Your original task was to call Jane to talk about a new line of copiers. Now that you've done that step, your next action step is to send Jane the link to the website so she can review more details about these copiers or maybe your next step is to send her a physical brochure so she can read about them. At this point, you have two choices: you can delete the original task and add a new one, or you can rephrase your original task. In either case, you'll describe your *next* action step and add or change the *Do Date* to reflect when you'll take that next action step. Either way is fine."

"OK, got it," Jim said. "But what if I *didn't* get a hold of Jane when I called her? What if I just left her a voice mail?"

"Well, if you didn't talk with her and you only left a voice mail, you'll want to follow up in a few days or in a week in case she doesn't call you back, right?" Holly asked.

"Yes," Jim said. "I'll still need to connect with her. So that task will stay on my list until I get a hold of her?"

"Exactly!" Holly confirmed. "And when we get to the topic of pending tasks and things you're waiting for we'll cover the best way to handle those kinds of scenarios. But for now, let's return to completed tasks. Since you said earlier that you were comfortable with deleting completed tasks, let's delete the *Check Box* column shall we?"

Jim agreed and Holly deleted the column.

"There you go," she said. "That's your new Task List. To recap, you have the *Due Date* column for your *Do Dates* or *Action dates* and the *Subject* column for your *Tasks* or *Action Steps*. And on the far left we're keeping the *Attachment* column, which we'll talk about later when we get into email. So that's all you need for now, but I'll add other useful features to your Task List after you start building the list. And now, your Task List is ready for some real tasks!"

Jim gave Holly a big smile. "I'm excited about this new Task List. I'm so ready to get rid of all my spiral pads, legal pads and the sticky notes around my monitor! I think this list will really help me stay focused and get things done!"

Chapter 5 Summary

- **Use your Task List for** *task management,* not *project management,* and focus on taking small action steps to move tasks forward.
- **The two most important questions to ask when planning tasks are:**
    - *What am I going to do?*
    - *When am I going to do it?*

  Your answers will address the "what" and "when" of getting things done.
- **Focus on when you'll** *do* **a task, not when it's** *due.*
- Enter your task in the *Subject* field and use the *Due Date* field for your *Do Date,* which is the date you plan to take action. This is the first level of priority for a task.
- Always determine if there is a **next action step** you need to take before deleting a task. If there *is* a next action step, either revise the original task or add a new task. Then add a *Do Date* to show your target date of action.
- **Delete tasks when they are** *truly* **complete**, with no further action steps. Don't accumulate *Completed Tasks* unnecessarily.

CHAPTER 6

Taking Control

"OK, JIM," HOLLY began, "it's time to start building your new Task List. I know you're eager to eliminate your stacks of papers, folders and legal pads and find where tasks are hiding." Holly and Jim switched chairs and settled in. "Where is your most recent to-do list on paper?"

"Right here," Jim said, pulling a legal pad off the top of a nearby stack. "I wrote this one up yesterday morning and I've been working from it since then."

"OK, good. First, in addition to looking for tasks, we're also looking for useful information that should be kept in other systems, like contact information that belongs in Contacts and appointment information that belongs on your Calendar. You might also find a page that can be torn off and filed in a file drawer. Once you finish reviewing a whole page from the pad and you move all of the information into other locations, you can tear off the page and toss it."

"OK, I'm ready!" said Jim. "Let's get started."

"First, check your to-do list and see what you've completed. Can you cross anything off?"

"Yes. I see a few things I can cross off right away," Jim said, drawing a line through several items.

"Great. Now, what's the first thing on the list you still need to do? Start at the top."

Jim read off his first task, and Holly asked him to summarize it. "OK, you can add this task to your Task List using the feature *Click here to add a new Task*, which will always show at the top of the list. You don't have to open the Task box. And remember to start your task with a verb." As she watched Jim enter the task, she noticed that he typed simply *Call Rebecca* and not the entire task he had just summarized for her.

"Jim, what about the rest? Remember to include all the details of the task you just summarized for me. Why are you calling Rebecca?"

"To get some more information about a new copier/scanner that my customer is interested in, but I think I'll remember that."

Holly gave Jim a look of caution. "Jim, when you finish building your new Task List, you're going to have quite a few tasks—possibly 30, 40 or even more, many of which will be planned for future days and weeks. Don't think that just because the details of a task are SO memorable today that you'll remember them later. I've seen my clients skimp on these details only to regret it later when the day arrives and they can't remember what they wanted to do, so they end up deleting the task. Remember, you have plenty of room to add details in the *Subject* field, so don't leave them out. More is more here, so be descriptive."

Jim nodded and added more details to his task. Holly asked, "And when would you like to call Rebecca?"

"Today," Jim responded.

"Then click on the drop-down menu and select today as your *Do Date*."

Jim selected the date, hit Enter and the task was added to the main Task List.

"Cool!" he said. "I like how easy this is." He continued to add tasks from the first page of his legal pad, including the verb, adding task details, and selecting *Do Dates*.

"Done," he said little while later. "I've reviewed everything on this page and entered all the tasks." At this point Holly checked the bottom left corner of his screen and could see that he had added fourteen tasks to his new Task List.

"Great job, Jim! Well done," Holly said. "Next you can…"

"Wait!" Jim said. "Can I add a few tasks I just remembered and don't want to forget?"

"Of course!" Holly agreed. She watched Jim add three more tasks, complete with *Do Dates* and good descriptions of the action steps.

"Great," Holly said. "That's a perfect way to use this list—for everything you don't want to forget to do, no matter when you want to do it." Holly looked closely at Jim's legal pad. "What about this one?" she said, pointing to a line in the middle that said *Multifunctional copiers – Reynolds Manufacturing.*

Taskology Tip #2

Build a single, digital Task List to consolidate and document everything you need to do so you can effectively plan and prioritize all tasks. (Not all in one day. All in one system.)

"Oh, right. I missed that one," Jim said. "I need to get some options together for Janet, the Purchasing Director at Reynolds Manufacturing. I need to do that today."

"OK," Holly said, "so what's your task? How, exactly, will you get the options together? Will you call a rep? Conduct research online? Check the information you have in your computer?"

"I'll call Jordan, one of our copier reps, to discuss the best options and get the process started. I want to make sure I haven't missed anything new that Janet might like to know about." Jim typed his task and entered a *Do Date* of today.

"Good. Now check the page again, Jim. Is there anything else you need from this page before you tear it off and toss it? A to-do, a reminder, any bit of information that might be useful to you? Look carefully. It's a very crowded page and I don't want you to miss anything."

After studying the page, Jim pointed to something written on the edge of the paper. "It looks like I wrote *Casey,* but there's no other information and I have no idea what that means." They both laughed.

"See?" Holly said. "That's why it's so important to actually spell out what you intend to do and when you want to take action. Then it's not just some little note hanging out there with no plan."

Jim crossed off the note. "I'm going to have to let that one go since I don't remember what that was all about. And at the bottom of the page I see the contact information for a new vendor."

Holly instructed him to add this information to his contact system. Once he finished entering the data, he enthusiastically tore the page off and tossed it into his recycle bin.

"Jim, it's the start of a brand new Task List. What do you think?" smiled Holly. She didn't really have to ask, since the excitement on Jim's face was obvious.

"Well, I gotta say… I'm pretty darn proud of myself! Eighteen new tasks, each one with verbs, details and target dates of action."

"Looks great, Jim!" Holly said. "Good job. You're in the process of being *S.A.V.E.D. by Your Task List!*"

"Saved by your Task List?" Jim asked with a laugh. "What does that mean?"

"S.A.V.E.D. is an acronym for the process you're doing right now. When you're *S.A.V.E.D. by Your Task List* it means you're typing a task with all of the necessary elements you need to actually get it done. **S** is for *Summarizing* your task. **A** is for your *Action step*. **V** is for the *Verb*. And the **E** and the **D** go together for *Enter* a *Date*."

"That's great, Holly," Jim said. "It's an easy process to follow that's really going to help me take control. I already feel so much better! Now, where do we go from here?"

"Let's continue with the next lesson as we talk about this list. Notice that you gave all eighteen tasks a *Do Date* of today or tomorrow."

Jim looked at his list. "I did, didn't I? Is that OK?"

"Well, I can tell you right now that nine or ten tasks per day is potentially unrealistic, especially since we haven't looked at your calendar yet to see what kind of time you have today to focus on these tasks. In addition, we've only just begun the process of capturing all of your tasks. There are so many more you have yet to find, and if you continue to add tasks for action today or tomorrow, your list will become even more unrealistic. A target of five or six tasks per day is a better way to begin."

Jim turned to Holly. "But I do way more than five or six things in a day!"

"You probably do, Jim, but first of all, some tasks are accomplished so quickly they never even make it to the list. Secondly, you've got to make sure that the tasks you *are* doing are the *right* things to do—your true priorities. Remember how you told me you've been feeling very reactive from day to day?"

Jim nodded in agreement.

"Well, this list will help you become more aware of your responsibilities so you can choose your priorities carefully. If lower priority tasks can wait a few more days, you'll be able to take action on your true priorities first. Today is the day you can start shifting from working *reactively* in your day to working more *proactively*. Then you're not jumping from one thing to the next all day without a plan. You see, I don't want you to *hope* that you'll get things done. This isn't a *wish list*. I want you to actually *get things done*."

"That would be great!" Jim said in agreement.

"Over the years," Holly continued, "I've found that planning five or six tasks is a great place to start. You may do more or less than that depending on the time you have available each day and depending on the *kinds* of tasks they are. Some may be five-minute tasks and others may take longer. But it's important to keep the number of tasks low, given all of the new tasks that will show up, plus the meetings, phone calls, and interruptions that occur all throughout the day."

"But I'm finding so many things I should have done *yesterday!*" Jim said in a distressed tone.

"I know you feel like you have some catching up to do, but no matter how many tasks you *try* to do, you still only have so many hours in a day. You may target doing ten tasks, but run out of time, and then you have to move them to a future date anyway. For now, you can target six or seven tasks if you want to, but keep an eye on how many you actually get to by the end of today, and let me know how it goes. As we talk more about time management and the role it plays in your task management, you'll get a better feel for what your daily targets should be."

"OK, I see what you mean," nodded Jim.

Taskology Tip #3

Your day will never be static and therefore your Task List will never be static. Your Task List will change to reflect new tasks and priorities, changes to existing tasks, and the deletion of completed tasks.

"And I want to make sure you don't feel trapped by your Task List or the plan you've set," continued Holly. "Your day will never be static so your Task List will never be static. Use this list as a tool for planning and reprioritizing, but understand that you'll continue to change it according to your *most* important priorities, which can appear at any time. That's the beauty of the list. It offers a solid plan of action, but it's flexible, too."

"Good. I definitely need flexibility, since things are constantly changing around here," Jim said.

"Now, before you target new *Do Dates* for some of these tasks," Holly said, "I want to take a minute now to add a new feature to your Task List that will help you with planning and prioritizing tasks each day." Holly proceeded to take Jim through the steps to group his tasks by *Do Date,* so each day was separate and tasks were totaled for each day. "Now you can more easily see what you've planned for each day," said Holly.

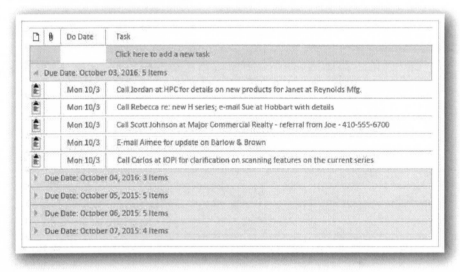

"Wow. That's great! That'll help me avoid loading up each day with too many tasks, right?" asked Jim.

"Right," Holly said. "But remember, if you have a bunch of quick calls or other small tasks, you can plan seven, eight or nine tasks for the day. Let's see how it goes."

Jim nodded. "I guess experience is the only way to find out."

"Exactly. As you continue planning and prioritizing your tasks, keep an eye on what you *actually* accomplish each day. It's important to remember that your success on any given day will depend on the nature of the tasks you plan and the time you have available. If your schedule is fairly open, you can plan to do five or six tasks—or maybe more, if they're quick tasks. But when your schedule is packed, you may only plan to do two or three.

"Next week, I'll ask you how you did. If you find you're not accomplishing the tasks you plan for each day, then plan fewer tasks, but if you consistently have time to spare, then target doing a few more. You won't know until you've had a chance to practice. What's *most* important is to identify your *top* priorities for the day and get those done—and feel *really good* about it —rather than risk missing your priorities, working reactively, and feeling *bad* because you didn't accomplish a much longer list."

Holly paused for a moment. "And don't worry about aiming too low. If you get through your tasks for the day and you get bored, you can always look at tomorrow's list." She chuckled and looked at Jim, as he joined in.

"Yeah, that's never going to happen around here. Should I move these tasks around now by selecting new *Do Dates*? I know I won't get to all of these today."

"Yes," Holly replied. "And one more thing before you move them. Tasks and time are tightly linked in the Taskology system, as they are in your workday. So your *Do Date,* your first level of priority, must be realistic. Look at your calendar *first* to be aware of your scheduled commitments before you target *Do Dates*. Otherwise your Task List could soon become very unrealistic. We'll get deeper into time management in a future appointment, but for now, get familiar with your calendar so you can plan realistically. I want you to have a good chance at actually accomplishing what you target. Let's go to your Calendar now and take a look at this week."

Jim clicked on his Outlook calendar and together they reviewed his scheduled meetings and calls for the upcoming week so Holly could estimate how many tasks he could target doing each day. She wanted Jim to learn the connection between his tasks and his time.

Taskology Tip #4
The Task-Time Connection

The number of tasks you plan to do each day should fit within the amount of time you have available. If you need more time, protect more time, but avoid planning to do more tasks than your time will allow.

"Now that we've looked at today and the next couple of days, I see that you have a little time to pursue maybe four or five tasks each day, depending on what kind of time they require. Let's prioritize your tasks now based on priority and time available. What are you *really* going to be able to do this afternoon? If you could only keep five tasks on today's list, which ones would they be?"

Jim went back to his Task List and reprioritized, leaving only five tasks for today and moving the rest to future days.

"That's more realistic," Holly said. "Doesn't that feel more achievable?"

"Yes. Actually, it does," Jim agreed. "I'm beginning to see how I can use this list to make a real plan I can feel good about."

"Good! And notice that with this new view, you can expand and collapse your list on each day, either by clicking on each day individually or by using the "Expand All Groups/Collapse All Groups" button on the tool ribbon under *View*. I recommend you collapse all days and then expand today, which allows you to focus *only* on today while ignoring future days. However, when you're reprioritizing periodically throughout the day, I recommend expanding your list to get a bird's-eye view of the next few days."

"This is great!" Jim said, following Holly's advice and compressing every day but today. "That's a nice feature. It feels much less distracting and less overwhelming when you don't have to see the rest of the list."

"Exactly. Now, let's see what else is in that legal pad of yours and we'll keep adding tasks to your new Task List."

Chapter 6 Summary

- **Build a single, digital Task List to consolidate and contain everything** you need to do so you can effectively compare and prioritize all tasks in one system. (Not all in one day. All in one *system*.)
- **Your day will never be static and therefore your Task List will never be static.** Your Task List will change to reflect new tasks and priorities, changes to existing tasks, and the deletion of completed tasks.
- **Detailed descriptions will support you best** when planning and prioritizing tasks. Always include *who*, *what* and *why* in the task description.
- *S.A.V.E.D. by Your Task List* is a tool to remember the necessary elements to include when planning tasks and adding them to your Task List.
  - **S** – *Summarize* your task
  - **A** – Identify your *Action step*
  - **V** – Start every task with a *Verb*
  - **E** – *Enter* a...
  - **D** – *Date*
- **Planning to do five or six tasks per day** is a good place to start before you learn how to manage interruptions and distractions, and learn how to protect more time in your day for getting things done.
- **The Task-Time Connection**
  The number of tasks you plan to do each day should match the time you have available. If you need more time, *protect* more time, but don't plan to do more tasks than your time will allow.

CHAPTER 7

Slow Down to Speed Up

As THEY PROCEEDED through the first hour of their appointment, Holly worked closely with Jim as he reviewed his legal pad, where he found meeting notes, contact information, notes from phone calls, tasks, and more. In addition to coaching Jim as he added tasks to his Task List, Holly showed him where to put useful information and how to make decisions about what's useful and what's not. When he finished going through his legal pad, and all the pages he'd written on had been filed or tossed, Holly gave Jim a high five.

"Congratulations! You've just eliminated your first legal pad!"

"It's a big day for me!" smiled Jim. "I'm feeling lighter and more focused already."

"Good! That's because you're beginning to free yourself from the challenges of using paper for to-do lists and reminders, and you're getting a lot more clarity about what's really on your plate."

After celebrating this notable achievement, Holly told Jim that it was time to tackle the papers and files on his desk and elsewhere in his office. They collected the random papers and files scattered across Jim's desk, credenza, conference table, and the floor and placed most of them on Jim's desk in separate piles, while a couple more stacks were placed on Jim's credenza.

Holly continued, "Paper *does* have a place in your workday, Jim, but only as a *tool*, not a *system*. When you use a pad of paper, it should be a temporary resting place for information, tasks or notes. When a call, conversation or meeting is over, you should move the information or the task to a more appropriate location for either reference or action. I'll show you what I mean as we find more legal pads and paper to-do lists today."

Holly pushed one of the stacks closer to Jim and she took the first folder off the top of the pile. "Let's start here, shall we? Tell me about this one."

"That's a file I'm working on for a customer," Jim explained. "I need to talk with Joe, our Service Manager, about a maintenance question on a particular series of copiers."

"Sounds like a task. Let's get it on the Task List. Are you going to call him, email him or visit his office? Be specific about what you're planning to do."

"I'll call Joe tomorrow and ask him my question." Jim added the task to his list, then asked what he should do with the file. Holly directed him to move it to an open area on his credenza and explained that they would use this area temporarily for the papers and files that were now represented on his Task List, but couldn't be tossed or filed.

Holly and Jim worked through the first pile and started on the second, with Holly guiding Jim through the process of decision making so he could determine which items could be filed, tossed, or delegated, or if the to-dos they represented should be added to his Task List. Somewhere near the middle of the second pile Jim picked up a glossy marketing folder and Holly asked him about it.

Jim quickly said, "Oh, that's just a folder of information I picked up at a conference earlier this year," and then he placed it on the other side of his desk.

Holly grabbed it and brought it back front and center. "Wait! You can't do that," she said with a big smile.

Jim looked up in surprise. "What do you mean? I'm not sure what to do with it."

"Exactly! But you need to make a decision on this. Decision making is essential to your progress, and the quickest way to stall your progress and create clutter in your office is to shuffle things around without making decisions. Remember this: *clutter* is collection of *unmade* or *deferred decisions*. If you put things aside without deciding how *useful* they are to you, you'll build a wall around yourself of unmade decisions. If you're not sure what to do with something like this," she said, waving the folder, "I'm here to help you decide."

Jim looked around his office. "I guess I've put a lot of things aside without making decisions, haven't I? I just didn't know what to do with them and I didn't feel like I had the time to figure it out."

"You're not alone... and that's why I'm here," Holly said with a reassuring smile. "I'll help you make decisions faster and easier. And as you already know, without the right systems to hold things and a process to make decisions, things will surely build up. But now you're changing all that and I'm going to talk you through it." Holly handed back the folder. "So what is this and how is it useful to you?"

Taskology Tip #5

Clutter represents a build-up of unmade or deferred decisions. Keep making decisions about everything you receive, whether physically or electronically.

"Well," he began as he opened it up, "it's a folder of information about a series of new high-end printers that I picked up at the last conference I attended, but I haven't checked it out yet."

"Could you or someone else on your sales team benefit from knowing about these new printers?"

"Not sure. I haven't looked through it so I don't know if it's a fit for anyone."

"Now, there's not a lot in here," Holly said, "so here's what I want you to do. Take sixty seconds to review the contents of the folder so you know something about this series of printers and you can decide who needs to know about it. Then I'll ask you my next set of questions."

Holly timed Jim and noticed that he reviewed the information and made a decision in less than sixty seconds.

"OK," he said, "I'll give this to Zach, one of my sales directors. His team serves hospitals and healthcare systems that may benefit from in this kind of high-end, specialty printer."

"Excellent," Holly said. "It took you less than sixty seconds to determine that, which illustrates my next lesson: *Slow Down to Speed Up*. When you *slow down* long enough to read or review something, then you can make a decision about it right away. And when you consistently make decisions, you can move things forward to the proper places for reference or action—or they're out of here. When you stick with this process, clutter won't build up, and in the long run you can *speed up* your productivity and progress."

"Slow down to speed up," Jim repeated. "It really didn't take long for me to figure out what I wanted to do with this, did it?"

"Not long at all. Based on what I've seen with other clients, you typically need between 30 and 60 seconds to make a decision, no matter what you're looking at. If you need a little more time to figure it out, and you have the time at that moment, do it, but if not, *it's a task.*"

"Oh! So if I thought I needed more time to read the contents of this folder in depth, I'd add it to my Task List—something like *Review marketing folder of new high-end printers from conference and determine who to speak to about it,* right?"

"Exactly! If it's worth an in-depth review and you might have a next action step, add it to your Task List. So, what are you going to do with this folder?" Holly asked.

"I'll put it in my Outbox and give it to Zach," Jim said. "Amazing. This is a huge breakthrough! With your help, I know I'll be much more productive. I think there are a lot of things in these piles that can be filed or tossed, and you can help me slow down long enough to make those decisions."

"I will!" Holly said. "And once you've practiced, you'll get into the habit of taking a minute to make decisions and then you can move on... *for good.*"

Jim picked up the next item off of the pile and groaned as he opened it up. "This folder is for Southpoint Savings and Loan. We're going back and forth on the terms and conditions, and I've had so many other things going on, I haven't gotten back to it yet. I really need to finish this up."

"OK, so what's your next action step?" Holly asked.

"Well, let me see here..." Jim flipped through the folder. "I need to revise certain clauses of the agreement and send it back to my customer, Janice, so she can review it and if they don't find anything else to question, they'll sign it."

"OK, then add that to your Task List," Holly said.

As Jim started entering his task, Holly decided to dig a little deeper. "Hold on, Jim. Do you know exactly what revisions you'll make to the agreement?"

"Well, I'd have to review the folder first," Jim said as he selected a *Do Date* for his task. "And then I need to check my email Inbox for her messages about the proposed revisions and see if we can do what she's requesting. I may need to talk with others about this or call her about the requested changes before I officially revise the agreement."

"OK, it sounds like you have quite a few things to do before you can revise this agreement and formally send it over to Janice to sign, correct?" When Jim nodded, Holly continued.

"Well, what you've added to your Task List is called a *dependent task,* which you want to avoid. The task you typed— *Make revisions to Southpoint agreement and send to Janice*—is actually *dependent* upon several other steps being taken first before you can make the revisions. It will be difficult for you to take fast action on this task, given that it's not actually describing your first step. So, which step will you take *first?*" Holly asked.

Jim thought for a second and answered, *"Review Southpoint folder and emails from Janice to identify the requested changes in terms and conditions."*

"Good," nodded Holly. As Jim revised his task, Holly continued the lesson. "A dependent task can really hold you up if you haven't identified the real next action step. You can end up procrastinating for several reasons. Usually it's because you know you have more work to do or steps to take before you can do the task as it's stated on your list. As a result, you'll sense more time is necessary and will put off the task until you have the time you need. At other times you may have stated it too broadly and need to narrow it down to just one small action step. When a task is properly identified, you can complete it without hesitation and then identify the *next* action step. Do you see the difference between how you entered it originally and the way it reads now?" Holly asked.

"Yeah, I do," Jim replied. "And if I'd left it as I originally wrote it, I probably would have put off the task even longer so I could knock it all out at once. But now I see there are several steps I need to take first, which is why this folder is still sitting here. Identifying the exact next action step will really help me get this done faster and easier."

"True," Holly said. "And you know how you mentioned you might have to call Janice about some of her requested changes? Well, don't add that step just yet, because you may not need to call her at all."

"Got it," Jim said as he put the file with the other papers and files that were represented on the Task List. Holly asked him what was next on the pile.

Jim held up a document. "I held on to this to remind myself that I want to talk about it at the next monthly Sales Meeting."

"Do you run that meeting and create the agenda, or does someone else?" Holly asked.

"Yes, I do both of those things," said Jim, "but I usually create the agenda at the last minute, right before the meeting."

Holly had a lot of helpful strategies for running effective meetings that she often passed along to her clients, but rather than get too far off track, she shared just a few of them with Jim, including when to provide agendas for upcoming meetings. She suggested that Jim add a task to his Task List for creating the agenda for the next meeting, well in advance of the meeting.

Jim typed *Create agenda for October Sales Meeting* and added a list of agenda topics in the *Notes* section of the task, which Holly explained was a good use of that field.

"Since you'll need this task every month, I call it an *evergreen* task," she explained. "You can simply move it from week to week prior to the next meeting and add agenda items in the *Notes* section. Those items will change each month as you remove topics that have been covered and add new ones to be discussed."

"Why not just make it a recurring task?" Jim asked. "I'd like to review this every Friday."

"Well, you can make it recurring if you'd like, but here's something to watch out for," Holly cautioned. "If you set this task to recur every Friday, but on a future Friday you're out at an all-day conference or on site at a client's office or in a lot of meetings that day, you're not going to see it. When that happens, that task is going to take a backseat. What I recommend is staying in charge of the task by *proactively* choosing the next, most realistic day you'd like to do or see that task, just like you would for any other task."

"Got it," Jim said. "I'll plan this task for Friday and then move it forward myself each week to whatever day is best."

"Good," Holly confirmed. "What's next on the pile?"

Jim took the next item off the top of the pile and then grabbed a few more. "These next couple of things are all different sales and dashboard reports. I can toss the old ones," he said, putting several reports in the recycle bin. "But I need to review these two. Should I put that on my Task List?"

"Here's a guideline you can use," Holly said. "Add a task to your Task List if it's going to take more than just a minute or two to review and make a decision OR if you're likely to take a next action step after reviewing it. The latter possibility is what I call *Review and Do*."

"*Review and Do?*" Jim asked. "What's that all about?"

"You see," Holly continued, "there are two different kinds of reading. Sometimes reading is just simple reading and once you've read it, you can toss it, delete it, file it or give it away. At other times, reading can be more of a *Review and Do* task, which means you'll read something and then you'll have a next action step to take, like creating a report or adding something to an agenda or sending an email to someone. This *Review and Do* kind of task really belongs on your Task List so you can make it a point to not only read what you need to read, but also to plan your next action step. Do you see the difference between simple reading and *Review and Do?*"

"Yes, definitely," Jim answered. "Most of what I need to do is just simple reading and then I can probably toss it or delete it, but sometimes I have a next step."

Jim proceeded to add *Review sales and dashboard reports* to his Task List. "I expect I'll need to take next action steps after reviewing these since I sometimes find discrepancies or have questions about the reports. I usually make a call or send emails after reviewing them."

"Sounds good," Holly confirmed.

As they finished off the second pile and started on the third, Holly noticed Jim was picking up speed. She often saw this type of progression with clients. Momentum tended to increase as decisions were made and things were filed, tossed or added to the Task List. She could tell that Jim was "in the zone," very focused and enjoying the process.

Chapter 7 Summary

- **Paper** is a tool, not a system. Save time and work more efficiently and effectively by using a digital Task List instead of writing and re-writing to-do lists on paper.
- **Clutter** is collection of unmade or deferred decisions. Keep making decisions about everything you receive, whether physically or digitally, and move things forward.
- **Slow Down to Speed Up**
  Slow down to read or review the items you receive so you can make decisions about what's useful to you and what's not. Move items you need to keep into better locations for reference or action, and dispense with items you don't need by tossing, archiving or deleting. Generally, it only takes 30-60 seconds to make quick decisions about what's useful to you and where to put it. When you slow down to review and make decisions, you can speed up your productivity and progress in the long run.
- **Dependent Tasks**
  A dependent task is one that requires one or more steps to be taken first and if entered into your Task List, it will hold up your progress. Identify and enter the real *first* or *next* action step on every task and when it's time to take action, you'll move forward without hesitation.

CHAPTER 8

Reach for the S.T.A.R.R.s

"I CAN ACTUALLY see my desk now!" Jim said with excitement. In just one hour he had cleared a large area of his desk, revealing a part of it he hadn't seen in a while. He was on a roll, making decisions quickly and clearing off stacks of paper and files. Plus, he'd added more than 30 tasks to his new Task List.

"Yes! Your progress is really impressive," said Holly, smiling. "Since you've already seen the many places where information can go and you've learned where to manage tasks, I want to tell you about one of my Productive Day® Quick-Start Guides called *Reach for the S.T.A.R.R.s.*"

"Uhhh, reach for the what?" asked Jim.

"*Reach for the S.T.A.R.R.s*," she smiled as she handed Jim a one-page document. "There are five places where things can physically go once they've entered your office, and the acronym—*S.T.A.R.R.*—outlines those locations. Put this somewhere where you'll see it every day for a while until this, too, becomes second nature. Are you ready?"

"Ready," Jim said as she handed him the document.

"First, *S.T.A.R.R.* is spelled with two Rs, and I'll get to those two Rs in a minute. Let's start with the S, which stands for *Send It Out*. This is a place for things you'll send out of your office, like mail, filing and things you'll delegate or give away. You already found plenty of things to send out today, and you have them in the proper place—in your Outbox on the far corner of your desk closest to the door so you can grab the contents on your way out. Actually, I even encourage clients to part with their Outboxes altogether."

Jim gave Holly a look of surprise. "Why?" he asked.

"Well, Outboxes give papers and files a cozy little place to stay—sometimes for too long—when really, the Outbox should be emptied regularly and often. Actually, many of my clients don't have physical Outboxes, so once that corner of their desk is clear, they just enjoy the open space. But you can keep your Outbox if you'd like," Holly said with a reassuring smile.

"Interesting," said Jim, intrigued by that possibility. "I think I'll do away with my Outbox, too, and see what it's like."

"Sounds good!" Holly said and continued with the acronym. "The T stands for *Toss it*—my favorite," she said with a big smile. "Now your trash can and recycle bin are in the right place, because they're under your desk. These bins should always be either under your desk or next to your desk, but not clear across the room. You wouldn't want to make it hard to toss things, because it you do, things will build up on your desk. And if you need to shred confidential documents, keep a bin handy for those, too.

"Then we have A for *Act on it*," Holly continued. "This refers to your *Action pile* or *Action file,* where you'll keep all the papers and files that represent tasks that are already on your Task List. This location will hold anything you need to keep until you finish a task, and you already have your *Action pile* right there," she said, pointing to the pile on Jim's credenza. "If you had an *Action file,* it would be a vertical sorter or a step file on your credenza—it wouldn't be tucked away in a file drawer. And as long as you choose *one* location for all of your *Action items* and stick with it, you'll have an easy way to manage the things that are showing on your Task List, OK?"

"Sure. Will I need to use a vertical sorter for my action items?" Jim asked.

"We'll see what you accumulate as you add more tasks to your Task List. Then I'll know what might work best for you," Holly replied.

Jim agreed. "And the two Rs? What do they stand for?"

"The first R is for *Reference*," Holly said. "The files in your desk, credenza and file cabinets will hold materials you'll need for future reference, and your files should be organized in a system you can trust and rely on."

Jim laughed. "I don't know if I trust my file cabinets. I tried to file something in there this morning,

Taskology Tip #6
Reach for the S.T.A.R.R.s

S – Send it out
T – Toss it
A – Act on it
R – Reference it
R – Read it

but look," he said, opening the right drawer of his credenza. "I can't even get my hand in there!"

"It's been a while since you looked for anything in there, huh?" Holly chuckled softly and reassured him that they'd address his files in a future appointment.

"The second R is for *Reading,*" she continued. "In this pile we'll put your reading collection, which might contain magazines, newspapers, trade journals, or things you've printed off the Internet to read. The reading pile will go on your credenza or on your conference table. Don't crowd your desk with a reading pile, because your desk should remain as open as possible and ready for focused work."

"I already have some reading right here," Jim said, pointing to a stack on his desk. "I might end up with a pretty big pile!" He grimaced.

"That's OK," Holly said. "I'll show you how to pare it down and how to manage it. And here's my tip about reading: be *really* selective about what you plan to read. Whatever you keep, you must read by the end of the week... *every* week. Any do you know why?

"No, why?" Jim asked.

"Because more reading is already on its way!" Holly laughed. "And if you don't keep up with it, you'll just accumulate it, but you won't gain any value from it."

"Got it. I'll choose my reading carefully," Jim said, nodding. "There are probably a few things in that pile I can toss."

"That would be great!" Holly said. "So that's the acronym *Reach for the S.T.A.R.R.s.* Oh, and one more thing," she added. "There's a flow to the physical information that enters your office. When it comes through the door, it will likely land someplace on your desk, but you don't want it to stall there. You need to review and make decisions quickly on each item you receive so you can keep it moving forward and get it into the right location for reference or action. Determine if it should go to someone else, get tossed, go into your reading pile, go into a file, or go on your Task List. These are all the locations represented by the letters in *S.T.A.R.R.*"

"OK, got it," Jim said. "When things land on my desk, I'll know what to do with them instead of just moving them aside and hoping I'll get back to them. And it just occurred to me that I should check out what's in my briefcase. I've been carrying around all kinds of things in there, including a bunch of reading."

"Oh, yes," Holly agreed. "Be sure to review what's in there and add anything you want to read to your reading pile. Be as selective and as realistic as possible, OK?"

"Don't worry," he replied. "I won't let my reading pile get out of control. With your help, I've finally managed to purge a lot of the clutter, and I have no intention of letting it build up again. This has been such a refreshing experience!"

Taskology Tip #7
Reading

Read what you set aside to read within the week you receive it, because more reading is already on its way to you. At the end of the week, if you still haven't read it, toss or delete it. You're not getting any value from it just by keeping it.

Jim felt a new sense of empowerment. He finally had a system and a process to take control of his paper, files and information, as well as a Task List to manage all of his tasks. The fog was beginning to lift, and he was finally getting some clarity back in his workday.

Chapter 8 Summary

- **Reach for the S.T.A.R.R.s:** an acronym to outline where to put items you receive each day in your office.
  - **S = Send it out**
  Just like an Outbox, this is a location on your desk where items can rest until they leave your office, which should occur several times a day. Outgoing items include things to mail out, give away, delegate, or file elsewhere. An actual Outbox is not necessary, but be sure to use a location on the far corner of your desk closest to the door.
  - **T = Toss it**
  Trash cans and recycle bins should be next to or under your desk. Shred bins should be nearby.
  - **A = Act on it**
  An *Action pile* or *Action file* is a location for the papers and files that represent tasks on your Task List while you're not working on them just yet. Keep items in a pile or in a vertical sorter on your desk or credenza, but not in your immediate work space.
  - **R = Reference it**
  Reference locations hold materials you want to reference in the future. Examples include file drawers in your desk and your credenza, or in the file cabinets in your office.
  - **R = Read it**
  The *Reading* pile holds physical reading materials, like magazines and newspapers, and should be kept on your desk or credenza, but not in your immediate work space. Reading should be read as soon as possible in order to gain value from it. Otherwise, it should be discarded. Protect time each week to read, and make sure it disappears by the end of every week, because more reading already on its way to you.

CHAPTER 9

What Are You Waiting For?

NEARING THE END of their second hour, Holly was thrilled with Jim's progress. She could see he was really getting into the system and changing the way he was thinking about getting things done.

"OK, Jim, it's time to tackle this step file," Holly said, taking the file from his credenza and placing it on his desk. "Tell me about these files and loose papers."

"Well, most of these things are pending. Either I'm waiting for something to happen or for someone to get back to me."

"OK, let's stop right here and talk about this," she said. "This is a danger zone I see a lot, so let me explain how to handle *pending tasks*." Holly pulled out a file folder and handed it to Jim. "Tell me about this file. Who or what are you waiting for on this one?"

Jim opened up the file and glanced at the contents. "Let's see... this customer's lease is up, so they wanted to upgrade all of their copiers and get a few new copiers, too. I'm waiting for the Purchasing Director, Sam, to let me know how many copiers they want to renew, plus which new copiers they want, and his confirmation of all the locations."

"And when was the last time you spoke with the Purchasing Director about this?"

"Hmmm... I'm not really sure. Maybe last week sometime," Jim said.

"So, what if Sam loses track of this and doesn't get back to you? Or he doesn't get back to you in a timely manner? What then?" Holly asked. "You can't always depend on other people to get back to you. Some people are very reliable, but others are not. *You* need to stay in control of your tasks so they don't slip through the cracks."

"You're right. I know I lose track of things like this because I'm so busy. So, should I add it to my Task List?" Jim asked.

"Yes. And here's why. *Pending* tasks and things you're *waiting for* always turn back into action for *you*, with very few exceptions. So don't separate things that are *pending* from your other tasks. They are ALL action steps that you'll need to take sooner or later. So let's put this on your Task List for today or tomorrow, because I assume you'd like to check in with Sam pretty soon, yes?"

"Yes, I should have heard from him by now. I'll call him later today," Jim said, entering the task on his Task List—*Call Sam about lease renewal, confirm copiers to renew, get new model numbers, confirm locations*—with a *Do Date* of today.

"Looks good, Jim," Holly said. "Now, let's say you call Sam again today, but you get his voice mail and you leave a message. How many days will you let pass before you call or email again?" Holly waited as Jim thought this through.

"I'll call him again tomorrow if I don't hear from him," Jim replied.

"Great. So, if you leave a voice mail this afternoon, keep the same task on your Task List and just change the *Do Date* to tomorrow, OK?"

"OK, got it. This list will really help to remind me of things that I don't want to forget about. This is great!" Jim said with a blend of enthusiasm and relief.

"And here's something else you can add to your task to help you keep track of the details." Holly paused to grab a pen she could use it to point at the screen. "At the end of the task in the *Subject* field, add a little note that says *lvm*, which stands for *left voice mail*, and add today's date. If you email someone, you can use *sem* for *sent email*. That way, you'll never forget the last time you reached out to someone with a call or an email because

---

Taskology Tip #8
Pending Tasks

"Pending" tasks or things you're "waiting for" almost always turn back into action for you. Add follow-ups to your Task List with a target date of action so nothing will be missed, lost or forgotten.

---

you'll have all the facts at hand. And feel free to add as many notes at the end of your task as you need. They can be very helpful in the long run."

"You mean, so I can ask someone why the heck they haven't gotten back to me?!" Jim asked.

"Yes, that could be one reason," Holly chuckled. "Especially if it's someone who really *should* have gotten back to you, like a team member or another key person in your line of business. But most importantly, having the facts at hand will help you make better decisions more quickly and accurately about when to take action again. It's hard to know what to do next or when to do it if you don't have a record of what you've already done. Without the facts, you have no idea where you are on this task—and that's not a powerfully productive place to be."

"It's true," said Jim. "In the past I've waited for someone to get back to me, but then I got so busy, I forgot all about it. Then I had to scramble to catch up and get it going again."

"Without a system or a process to follow, it's easy to forget follow-ups," Holly said. "Setting things aside in a *waiting for* file or a *pending* pile is danger-ous, but you can avoid that danger by using your Task List and a process like this. Also, having all the facts will help you prioritize faster when your days get a little crazy. If higher priorities pile up today, you can quickly and easily decide whether or not to wait another day or two to follow up with someone when you already know you just reached out to someone yesterday. Keeping track of what you've done makes it easier to prioritize and act quickly, with more accuracy and confidence."

"Let me make sure I have this right," said Jim. "If I don't catch up with Sam this afternoon, I should put *lvm* and today's date at the end of the task, and then change the *Do Date* to tomorrow so I'll see it again. Is that right?"

"Yes, exactly," Holly confirmed. "And if you *do* hear from Sam before tomorrow, just locate the task on your list and change it according to the out-come of your conversation."

"I have plenty of *pending* tasks in this step file and probably a few more in some of these other stacks of papers and files." Jim said, looking around. "Of course, I'm not sure where they all are…"

"Well, we'll find them all and incorporate them into your Task List. You'll get lots of practice on *pending* tasks!" Holly said.

Jim and Holly continued reviewing Jim's step file until they emptied it. After Jim added the last task onto his Task List he flopped back in his chair with satisfaction and grinned at Holly.

"Look at that Task List, Jim…more than 40 tasks! You should be very proud of yourself!" said Holly.

"Yeah, I do! And I feel great about this list," Jim said, his excitement showing. "It's really going to help me stay on top of my game."

He decided to use the now-empty step file for all of the papers and files that were represented on his Task List. He began sorting things into the various sections as Holly looked on. "Can you suggest an order for all this stuff?" he asked.

"It's up to you," she said. "There's no special order. Just keep loose papers in the first section in front of the folders so you can always see them. And don't try to over-organize it. For instance, don't try to put it in order by *Do Dates*. That's too high-maintenance."

"Good tip," Jim nodded. "I may need another vertical sorter to hold all of my *Action items*, but I can't begin to tell you how relieved I feel! I've eliminated so much clutter today and tamed most of the chaos. This system is really going to help me stay in control of my day!"

Chapter 9 Summary

- **Pending tasks** or things you're "waiting for" almost always turn back into action for you. If you set these items aside in a pending pile or "waiting for" file and expect others to follow up, you could lose progress. Add tasks to your Task List to remind you to follow up on anything you're waiting for so tasks won't stall or slip through the cracks.
- **Keep track of how and when you follow up on tasks.**
  Add "lvm" for "left voice mail" at the end of the task and add the date you left the voicemail. Use "sem" for "sent email." These notations will remind you of how and when you last reached out to someone and will be helpful when:
  - You would have otherwise forgotten when and how you last reached out.
  - You're planning how much time to give someone to get back to you before taking action again.
  - Your days get busy with new priorities, issues or emergencies and having the facts at hand helps you prioritize and act more quickly.

Prioritize with Precision

AFTER A COUPLE of hours working with Holly, Jim was energized by his progress. Finally he was beginning to feel like himself again. "I can't believe how much stuff we've sorted out already," he said, pausing to smile at Holly. "You've helped me make so many changes in such a short amount of time."

"But wait, there's more," Holly said with a big smile. "We're going to take this list a step further."

"More?" Jim laughed. "All right! Bring it on!"

"Now I'm going to show you how to prioritize *within* a day." Holly borrowed the mouse and started adjusting his screen. "You already know that the first level of priority for your tasks is determined by your *Do Date* or date of action. Something you target doing today is more imperative than something you'll do next month. That's all about timing. The second level of priority will help you determine the *value* of your tasks and you'll be able to see the most important tasks at the top of your list each day."

"So, I'm going to rank my tasks?" Jim asked.

"No, not ranking them individually, like 1, 2, 3, 4, 5, 6, 7... This is a different approach," Holly said. "We're going to add a priority column to your Task List where you'll add the numbers 1, 2 or 3 to define the *meaning* or *value* of each task. This number will answer the question: *What role does this task play in my day?*"

Jim asked, "OK, I'm ready. What are the definitions for 1, 2, and 3?"

"1 is for *revenue-generating* tasks. These are *money-makers* or *business-builders*. Or they can be *money-savers* if your role is saving money for the company. These tasks represent the very the *best* use of your time. A 1 could also represent a very *urgent* matter that's not a money-maker, but in general, think of your 1s as *revenue generators.* For example, 1s would include calling prospects and customers or any step that helps you move the sales process along."

"OK, got it," Jim said. "What's a 2?"

"A 2 simply means *important*," Holly explained. "It's a task that's part of your job and keeps the wheels turning on the business, but it doesn't qualify as a 1 because it doesn't necessarily bring in revenue and it's not urgent. For you, 2s would include creating your sales meeting agendas, collaborating with your team on projects, reviewing reports, working with Jennifer, or calling other people at Octagon about various company initiatives."

"OK, and what's a 3?" Jim asked.

"3s are for tasks that would be *nice to do*. They're not important or urgent tasks, but *it would be nice if I could do that today* or *read this today* — that sort of thing. As a general rule, *most* tasks on a Task List should be 2s so the 1s stand out and the 3s stand out. And you don't want too many 1s because then *everything* is a priority, and you know what happens when everything is priority, right?" Holly asked.

"Uh… I'm not sure," Jim said, hesitating.

"If *everything* is a priority, then *nothing* is a priority," Holly answered with a smile.

"Ah, yes. That's true," Jim agreed.

"Now it's time to enter a 1, 2 or 3 for each task on your Task List, using the column I added."

"For all of them?" Jim asked.

"Yes," Holly said. "Defining the *meaning* or the *value* of each task will help you compare them and make decisions about your priorities. You want to have as much information as possible to help you prioritize from moment to moment, no matter what kind of day you're having. Only filling in *some* of these numbers won't save you any time." Holly paused for a moment. "Here's a pop quiz for you… when your day gets crazy, which kind of task should be the first for getting reprioritized for another day…a 1, a 2 or a 3?"

"Definitely the 3s," Jim said without hesitation.

"Yes, most definitely the 3s, because you've already determined that these tasks would only be *nice to do*."

Jim proceeded to enter 1s, 2s, and 3s for all of his tasks and then sat back in his chair and viewed the list. This process definitely put a finer point on his Task List and gave him a whole new level of prioritization. "I'm just thinking about these numbers. Can a 2 become a 1?"

"Yes," Holly said. "But only because too much time has passed and the task is now urgent. It's not because it suddenly became a money-maker. Usually a 2 will become a 1 because you're nearing a deadline or running out of time. The same goes for a 3 becoming a 2. If you procrastinate on a 3 and you still need to do it, it could become a 2 because too much time has passed."

Taskology Tip #9
Taskology Priorities

1 = Revenue-generating
2 = Important
3 = It would be nice if...

Jim nodded his head in understanding. "This is great. It's so different from any approach I've ever tried before. And it's so easy!"

"Excellent! I'm glad you like it, Jim!" Holly beamed.

They continued to process the papers and files from the remaining stacks and managed to get through most of it by the end of the third hour.

Jim stopped and looked around his office. "I can't believe how much we accomplished today!" he beamed. "I was sure those papers and files had grown roots everywhere they sat, but they're almost gone!" He swept his arm across the room. "Open space is such a beautiful sight."

"I'm so pleased with all you did today and how you're feeling now, Jim," Holly said. "Since our first appointment is nearly over, let's take a few minutes to talk about how to use your Task List from day to day."

"First," she began, "this Task List is what I call *Mission Control*. It shows everything you need to do all in one system, with some tasks planned for action today and the rest are planned for future days. Look at your list first thing in the morning and periodically throughout the day to see what you've done and not done, and reprioritize as necessary. Add new tasks as they come up and adjust tasks that need a new next action step and a new *Do Date*. And you can delete tasks that are completely finished if there are no further action steps. Keep using your list and it will keep supporting you. But, like any system, if you stop supporting it, it will stop supporting you. Then you'll lose the clarity and control you're creating in your workday right now."

Jim was listening intently, leaning back in his chair. As soon as Holly paused, he jumped in with a question that had been growing in his mind. "Holly, how much time will I spend each day maintaining this list?"

"Well, the biggest and most powerful investment of time, by far, is in the beginning when you build the list, and you're almost finished with that phase. Once the list is fully built, you'll just continue to use it daily, and there's no real maintenance. Just keep the list accurate and up to date so it truly reflects what you want to do and when you want to do it."

"Good," Jim said. "I want to make sure I'm spending my time on *task management*, not *list management*."

"I can assure you," Holly began, "that this is all about *task management* and you won't get "lost in the system," meaning you won't be color coding, categorizing, over-organizing or playing with all the bells and whistles that many systems offer for their to-do lists. Remember when I said that Taskology was created to simplify task management?"

"Yes," replied Jim.

"Well, I've seen other software programs and methods out there where a person can get so distracted by all the ways they can organize their tasks that they never actually get anything done! And when that happens, they're getting lost in the system and losing time instead of *working* the system and getting things done. But that's not going to happen to you because we've already set up your list so it's simple, logical and easy to use. You only need to focus on the two most important things for getting things done. Do you remember what those are?"

"Let's see—what I'm going to do and when I'm going to do it?" Jim asked, as Holly nodded. "And how many times a day should I look at my list?"

"A couple of times in the morning, a couple of times in the afternoon, and especially after you've just completed a task. As you saw today, it takes only seconds to add, change or delete tasks, as well as reprioritize them. And when you need to reprioritize your tasks, you'll look at your list for today and the next couple of days, but you should never have to reprioritize your *whole list*, which includes tasks for action in future weeks or months."

Jim nodded. "That all sounds very manageable. What about my list for tomorrow? Should I review and prioritize it first thing in the morning? Or do it today before I leave?"

"Definitely review your list for tomorrow by the end of today. Unless you receive an emergency call on your way to work in the morning, you should be able to just open your Task List for the day and get started."

"So, to recap," Holly continued, "by the end of each day, make sure *all* tasks for that day are reprioritized or deleted. If you've finished a task, and there are no further action steps, simply delete the task. But if there *is* a next action step, make sure you document it. Rephrase the original task so it reflects the new action step and then change the *Do Date*. And if you didn't get to a task, just reprioritize it for another day. When you keep your list up-to-date by following these steps throughout the day you should have no tasks showing by the end of the day."

"What if I forget to look at the list? Can I print it out?" Jim asked.

"I don't recommend printing the list, Jim," Holly said. "If you print it, you'll make double work for yourself, because you'll write on your list, but then you'll have to update it in the computer anyway. The whole point of using a digital Task List is to make it easy to access, read, update, and prioritize—all in an instant—and you can't do that quickly or easily on paper. And once all of your papers and files are gone, it'll be easier for you to remember to look at your Task List. Soon—and especially after we address email—you won't have anywhere else to look!"

"I can't wait!" Jim said. "One more question... what about using task reminders?" asked Jim.

"Those aren't necessary in Taskology, Jim, and I'll tell you why," Holly answered. "When those are used, they pop up constantly, which is a reactive and *unproductive* way to manage your day, and you'll end up dismissing them all day long instead of getting things done. Rather than rely on task reminders to *push* tasks at you, be proactive and *pull* from your list as you look at it all throughout your day. Remember, you've built this list with all the things you said you wanted to do, so look at it and use it. When you keep your list in good shape, it will always support you and never let you down."

"And if my day gets completely turned upside down, I shouldn't feel bad about moving tasks around?" asked Jim.

"Not at all," Holly said. "Remember that your day will never be static and therefore your Task List will never be static. As your day changes— and *it will*—your priorities will change and your list must reflect those changes. Usually, your workdays won't get completely turned upside down, but things will come up and you'll have to regroup. On a typical day, let's say you check your list around 3 o'clock and see there are four tasks remaining. You'll look at your calendar and assess how much time you have for these last few tasks. If you realize you won't get to them all, reprioritize the ones you *won't* get to and leave the one or two you'll do. This process will keep your list accurate, up to date and very meaningful."

"And if something comes up that I can't do immediately—because I don't want to be too reactive," Jim said, hoping to get credit for thinking more pro-actively, "then I'll add it to my Task List right away, right?"

"Right," Holly said. "You'll regularly compare what's on your list with everything new that comes up. This list gives you the power to decide—*pro-actively*—what your priorities are at that moment, and what you'll do next and why. You're in the driver's seat of your workday— not in the back seat or the trunk!" Holly said with a chuckle.

Jim laughed too, getting a visual of Holly's metaphor.

"Here's an example," Holly continued. "Let's say you get a call today from a big prospect who's ready to sign a contract worth $250,000 and that means a next step for you. That next step is an important task. This list gives you the ability to compare that task with everything else you had already planned to do today so reprioritize if necessary. You may bump a task originally planned for today in light of this new one. You see, Jim, this Task List is not just about *what you plan to do*. It's also about what you *choose not to do*. You get to decide where your time goes, and if a task gets moved to another more realistic date, it's safe. The tasks you choose NOT to do won't be forgotten."

"Got it," Jim said. "That's really going to help me when my day is moving fast and I need to make quick decisions. And I won't forget anything I move to a future date." Jim paused for a moment. "So, I have another question. What if I move a task forward more than once? Is that considered *procrastinating?*"

"Aha!" Holly laughed. "It all depends. If a new priority pops up and you need to move a few tasks to accommodate it, then you're simply reprioritizing, which is good. However, if you continually move the same task to a later date—again and again—it's time to find out why."

"Ask yourself," Holly continued, *"Am I stalling because the task was stated too broadly and not as a small action step?* We already talked about situations where a task may be missing a verb or important details, and we also talked about *dependent* tasks, which can easily cause you to procrastinate."

"Yes," Jim agreed. "Like before when I had a string of steps I needed to take first that weren't identified and I could have easily procrastinated, knowing I needed more time to do the task as I had typed it originally. And then I boiled it down to my real first action step."

"Right," Holly confirmed. "Plus, there will be times when you can delegate. You may see a task that shouldn't be on your list at all because Jennifer could do it—or perhaps someone else on your team."

"Yes, I'll look out for those, too," Jim replied.

"Reflecting on these different scenarios will help you understand why you might be procrastinating on something and continually moving it to a future date."

"In the past, I know I've let things stall, but it was usually because I just forgot about it!" Jim said. "But now, it'll be clear to me what's going on. I'll know right away if I'm procrastinating. This Task List will be very helpful. And no one is going to believe what my office looks like now!" He spun his chair around to admire his almost clutter-free office.

Holly laughed. "Have fun showing it off and enjoy the open space! They'll probably ask you if you're leaving. That's what I hear from my clients after an appointment like this. Meanwhile, what I'd like you to do in the coming week is work through the remaining papers and files when you can and keep adding tasks to your Task List. Keep using the list and keep adjusting tasks as you get things done and as your day changes. Delete tasks when they are *truly* complete, and remember to capture all next action steps, OK? Next time we'll focus on time management."

"OK!" Jim said. "I'll be ready. Thank you so much!"

Chapter 10 Summary

- **Prioritize tasks within each day by using a 1, 2 or 3 to designate meaning or value.** Most tasks should reflect 2s. The 1s should stand out and the 3s should stand out. When too many tasks have 1s, it means everything is a priority, and then nothing is a priority.
  - o **1 = a revenue-generating,** money-making, money-saving, or business-building task. Or this could be a task that's terribly urgent. Overall, a task that gets a 1 is the BEST use of your time.
  - o **2 = an important task.** These tasks are requirements of your job. They must be accomplished and keep your daily business moving forward.
  - o **3 = "It would be nice if..."** These tasks would be *nice to do.* These are tasks that aren't time sensitive or of high importance. This kind of task may include certain kinds of reading, video watching, and ideas to consider.
- **ALL tasks (not just some tasks) receive a 1, 2 or 3** so you can instantly recognize the value, meaning or importance of a task, which will help you prioritize with more efficiency and accuracy. Using these will help you ensure you get the right things done at the right time.
- **A 2 can become a 1 and a 3 can become a 2 because of the passage of time or a looming deadline ahead.** When a 2 becomes a 1, it doesn't mean it suddenly became a money-maker, but rather it just became more urgent due to a time constraint. The same applies when a 3 becomes a 2.
- **Your Task List is *Mission Control.*** It holds everything you need to do in one system. Review your list periodically throughout the day to see what you've done and not done, and reprioritize as necessary. Take time to add, change and delete tasks from the list, and adjust tasks that need a new next action step and a new *Do Date.* When you see you're running

out of time to accomplish everything on your list for the day, the 3s are the first to be moved.

- **By the end of each day, make sure *all* tasks for the day are reprioritized or deleted.**

  If a task is NOT completed by the end of the day, reprioritize it for a more realistic day in the future. If you identify a next action step for a task, rephrase the original task to reflect the new action step and give it a new *Do Date*. If you finish a task, and there are no further action steps, simply delete the task.

CHAPTER 11

Getting Noticed

"HEY, BUDDY! YOU leavin' us?" Mike Walters laughed as he leaned against the doorway to Jim's office. Mike was the CFO for Octagon Office Solutions and he considered Jim a close friend.

"Ha! No..." Jim chuckled as he turned away from his computer to face Mike. "No, I'm working with a productivity consultant. She's showing me how to be more productive, which means I'm getting organized, too. So, what do you think of my office? Not bad, huh?"

"Yeah, it looks great," Mike said, taking a closer look. "My office hasn't looked like this since my first day with the company."

"Then you should spend some time with this consultant," Jim said. "Your office could look like mine!"

"Intriguing... but not likely. Have you seen my office lately?" Mike laughed, walking into Jim's office. "So, what type of things is this consultant teaching you?"

"Better workload management. We built my new Task List this morning and, in the process, I'm getting really clear about what's on my plate."

"A Task List, huh?" Mike said. "Show me what you're talking about." He walked around the desk and looked over Jim's shoulder at his computer.

"Here it is. Since I have Microsoft Outlook, that's where we built my list. I knew this option was here, but I'd never used it before," Jim said.

"I tried using the Task List in Outlook a long time ago," said Mike, "but it didn't work for me, so I gave up."

Jim nodded. "Holly, my consultant, told me that a lot people say that, because they don't know *how* to use a list like this—no matter what kind of software they have. She said that without a methodology to follow, it's hard to make *any* task list work. So she helped me set up this one according to her system, Taskology, and now that I understand how to use it, I have to say it's awesome."

"Huh. Interesting," nodded Mike. "Good to hear it's working for you. What did you say her system is called?"

"Taskology, and the Task List is the first thing you learn." Mike listened as Jim gave him a quick run-down of the Taskology Task List and how it works. "For years I used to use legal pads and notebooks and papers and files to remind me of everything I needed to do, but now I have just this ONE list—where ALL of my tasks are consolidated—and it's already helping me focus more on what I need to do."

Mike walked back around Jim's desk and sat in one of the guest chairs. "I don't know, Jim," he said slowly, mulling over what Jim had just told him. "It's great that you found something to help you...but give up on paper? I don't know...I'm really attached to paper and I like my spiral notebook. I put everything in there and it keeps me on track."

"Well, do you ever miss things or lose track of things to do in your notebook?" asked Jim.

"Yeah... maybe... sometimes," replied Mike. "But that's not the only way I keep track of things to do. I have plenty of other methods, just in case I do lose track—especially for the really critical stuff."

"Let me guess... you have papers and files sitting on your desk to remind you of things to do. And I bet you use sticky notes, too, right?" Mike was nodding as Jim was speaking. Jim smiled and continued, "Do you also keep a list in your head?"

"Yep, I use all of those things. I use sticky notes for the important to-dos and keep current files on my desk. I know exactly where everything is, so it all works for me," Mike shrugged. "I get what you're saying, but I'm not sure I need to make any changes. You know...why fix it if it's working?"

"I bet you also have emails in your Inbox to remind you of things to do, don't you?"

"Of course. Don't we all?" Mike asked as he secretly wondered if maybe that *wasn't* the best way to manage email. Clearly, Jim had found a system he loved and wasn't about to give up on the possibility that Mike could benefit from it, too. Mike continued, "The emails are in my Inbox, but I also print them and put them on my desk so don't lose track of them."

Jim nodded. "I'd been printing emails too, but Holly says I don't have to do that anymore. The to-dos from email will be incorporated into the Task List now."

"Really?" Mike asked. "Interesting. I didn't think that was possible."

"Yeah, that'll make a HUGE difference. You know, Mike, everything you do today sounds a lot like what I used to do. Until Holly helped me build this list, I was using all kinds of ways to keep track of things to do, and I didn't realize how difficult I was making it to keep up. Holly says it's impossible to successfully manage and prioritize to dos from each of their individual sources, and that consolidation is the key. We pulled tasks from my legal pads, my sticky notes, my notebook, my head, my papers and files…it was almost comical to realize all of the stuff I was using for reminders!"

Mike slowly nodded. Sure, the new system had some advantages, but his notebook and his printed emails were working for him—so why change? And even if he DID want to change, where would he find the time to learn a whole new system? "Yeah, you're right. I do use lots of different ways to keep track of things to do, but the bottom line is that I know what I need to do each day, and I get things done. Sure, I might miss a few minor things from time to time, but ---"

"---but why miss *anything*?" Jim interjected. "With this new list I now have a plan of action that makes sense… and it's actually doable. Plus, as Holly and I addressed my stacks of papers and files, we found a whole bunch of things I could file, toss, or give away. I'm already so much more organized than I was when I came in this morning!"

"Yeah, it looks fantastic in here," Mike said, looking around Jim's office. "I noticed you don't have any stacks of paper anymore." The stacks of paper in his own office seemed to have multiplied lately, but only because he hadn't had time to go through them. He knew he'd get back on track . . . eventually. "My office isn't nearly as neat, but I know where everything is. I can put my hands on anything I need," Mike said with a confident smile.

Jim nodded. "Yeah, but how much time are you spending looking for papers or files in those stacks?"

Mike let out a sigh. Jim had hit a sore spot. "Well, yeah… it takes a little time to find things these days." Mike hated wasting time and he'd grown impatient with all the time he'd lost searching through the piles on his desk for things he needed right away, but he wasn't about to admit all of that to Jim.

"You could probably save time if you used a handy Task List to keep track of things to do instead of leaving reminders all over your desk. And you could probably save time using a reliable file system to hold all the reference materials you need to keep… and find fast. As I recall, your desk looks a lot like mine used to," Jim teased.

Mike made a face and shook his head. "Yeah…OK… my desk definitely doesn't look as good as it used to." And he thought silently …*and it definitely doesn't look as good as this one.*

"And speaking of getting time back," Jim continued, "I'm so clear about what I need to do now that I won't waste any time trying to figure out what to do from moment to moment. I used to waste SO much time reviewing things again and again to see where I was, and to see what I'd done or not done. I'd have to start from scratch every time, writing new to-do lists. But now I won't have to go through a whole review process to figure out what I need to do next. My plan is already in my Task List and I can just dive into the next task and get going."

"Which is great," Mike agreed, "but your plan could change, right? I mean, what if something comes up that you *didn't* plan?"

"Of course!" Jim responded. "I'm always going to add new tasks that show up and reprioritize others, and I'll delete tasks when they're completely finished. Then when a new task shows up that I didn't anticipate, I can quickly decide whether it's a priority and I should jump on it now—compared to the other tasks I had planned—or just add it to my list for later and finish up what I was already working on. These are the perks of this new Task List: I can turn on a dime, reprioritize in an instant, stay in control of ALL of my tasks, and nothing will slip through the cracks."

Mike stopped and thought for a moment. Jim's enthusiasm was a bit over the top, but Mike was starting to understand why. He had to admit he liked what he was hearing. But, realistically, did he have time to learn a new system? He already felt buried.

"So, how long does it take?" Mike asked, not sure of the payoff yet. "How much time will you spend with Holly to learn the system and what do you have to do *after* working with her?"

"Holly said that the biggest investment of time is up front in building the Task List. It'll take a couple of hours, but at the same time you'll get 100% clarity of what you're responsible for, reduce the clutter in your office, save time, and start making more progress. It's like hitting a few birds with one stone."

"Hang on. Let me get this straight," Mike interjected. "You build the Task List and clear off your desk at the same time?"

"Yep," smiled Jim. "Holly and I did all this in one morning."

"Seriously? In one morning?" Mike asked in disbelief.

"Yep," Jim said as he smiled. "It's so cleansing to get rid of all of the *stuff* and get a plan in place for everything you need to do. And Holly said that after the list is built, you'll just spend a little time each day using the list—adding to it, changing it, and deleting from it – to keep it accurate and up-to-date. And she said that would be true for any system—you have to use it in order to keep it meaningful to you."

Mike listened intently and nodded as Jim talked.

"The time spent is SO worth it," Jim continued. "I already feel SO much better. And because I'm not overloading each day with fifteen or twenty things to do, it only takes seconds to reprioritize the list and change my plan."

"Reprioritize or procrastinate?" Mike asked jokingly.

"Funny..." Jim said. "Reprioritize. Holly said today that the list helps in two ways. It's not only great for helping me do the things I said I wanted to do, but it's also great for tracking the things I can't do this minute—the things I choose *not* to do. Plus, I can focus on what I want to do today, and not worry about the things I don't need to do until next week. And, I like that I can also prioritize *within* a day, so I can see the hottest priorities at the top of the list."

"Definitely sounds good," Mike said, nodding. "And she said you could include email in the list? With what... the flags?"

"Apparently, the flags aren't used in Taskology, but I'll find out more when Holly shows me, and then I won't have to print emails anymore! I can't wait.

And I'm really looking forward to getting my email Inbox down to zero," Jim said with a smile.

Mike focused his attention on Jim. Had he heard that correctly? "You can get your Inbox to zero?"

"Yep. Sure can. That's what Holly's telling me and I'm all for it. I'm so tired of being buried in email."

"Yeah... tell me about it," Mike said, letting that idea sink in. An empty Inbox? It sounded too good to be true. "But email is pouring in *constantly*. How is an empty Inbox even possible? And is getting to zero even necessary? We've got plenty of space on the server."

"Well, think about it," Jim began. "Email builds up in the Inbox and then scrolls off the screen, but important things are scrolling off the screen. Sure, we have room on the server, but the bigger concern is what people are *missing*—what they're losing or forgetting—and how much time they're *wasting* reviewing flagged emails again and again and again. And even if you do catch certain to-dos from emails, how are you going to prioritize them with everything else you need to do when they're sitting in the Inbox?"

"Yeah, but what kind of time is it going to take to get to zero? That's a lot of email for most people, including me." Mike wasn't yet convinced it was realistic, but he wanted to hear the rationale.

"According to Holly, getting to zero is hugely important to our productivity, and it's a necessary step if we really want to stay in control of our workload without losing track of tasks and information. She said the Inbox is a tool to bring emails IN, but they should go back out again to better places of either reference or action. It requires an investment of time up front, yes—just like building the Task List—but once the system is in place, it's easy to get emails where they need to go, which are all places *outside* of the Inbox. I think most people are like me, and they don't have anywhere to put the emails or the information that come from emails. And without a system in place to make it easy, email piles up in the Inbox."

"That's for sure," agreed Mike, reflecting on the size of his own Inbox. He was also intrigued by the idea that he could combine to-dos from a variety of sources—including email—into one Task List and keep track them all in one place. He tried to imagine what that would be like.

"*And,*" Jim said, "Holly also said that if I had any *Rules* in place for rerouting my emails—which I do—that I'll probably get rid of them. But first we're going to review how I'm using *Rules* and then decide what to do."

"I'm surprised to hear you'll get rid of your *Rules,*" Mike said. "I thought using *Rules* was the best way to manage emails and stay organized."

"Well, Holly said that using *Rules* can actually *hurt* your productivity, because it channels emails into folders without taking into consideration the amount of time you need to read or review them. Email gets filtered out of the Inbox and sent into folders that many people don't go back to review. They think they'll review them later, but *later* never comes—and that's certainly happened to me," Jim said. "She mentioned that a lot of people lose information and miss deadlines when they use *Rules.*"

Mike thought for a moment about his use of *Rules.* He wasn't sure if he wanted to do away with them, but could understand why they could spell trouble.

"Well, Jim, you've given me a lot to think about," Mike said. "It's great that you found this new system, and I'm intrigued by what you told me. I'm going to take stock of my day and see what's sitting on my desk as reminders of things to do. And I can't believe I'm saying this, but I might re-evaluate how I'm using my spiral notebook, too." He got up from the guest chair and headed out of Jim's office.

"I'd recommend it!" he heard Jim call out.

Protecting More Time

BY THE TIME Holly returned a week later for their second appointment, Jim couldn't wait to show her the progress he'd made. He greeted her in the lobby, walked her to his office and opened his office door with a dramatic flourish.

"Look what I did between our appointments! When we finished last week there were still a couple stacks of paper and files on the right side of my desk, but now they're gone! I finished off the pile on the credenza, too, and then tackled the last pile on the other side of my desk."

"Excellent job, Jim!" Holly said. "I'm so proud of you! You must be feeling so much better, and you're office looks great."

Jim smiled. "Thanks! I'm really pleased with all the progress I've made in just a week."

"And how's it going with your Task List?"

"Very well, I think," answered Jim. Holly stood behind him as he sat down at his computer and showed her his Task List. "I look at my list all throughout the day—adding new tasks and deleting ones I've finished. Then I change some of them and give them new *Do Dates*. I'm also trying to keep an eye on what I'm planning and what I get to and what I *don't* get to. This list has really helped me stay on top of things. I feel calmer, more in control and more focused."

"That's great, Jim! Your list looks really good. You haven't left any tasks on prior days, and I see you're using your priority numbers 1, 2 and 3." Then Holly paused and looked at his list more closely. "Today and tomorrow look slightly heavy, though, with the number of tasks you've planned, but all in all, I'd say you've had a very successful first week. Congratulations!"

"Thanks," Jim said. "I can definitely do a bit better with planning, but I feel really good just having this list. I'm far less worried that I'm going to miss something."

Leslie Shreve

"Good," Holly smiled. "I'd like to address the number of tasks you've planned for each day, but first I want to share a lesson in time management—something many professionals struggle with."

"And I'm one of them," said Jim.

"OK. First click on your Calendar so we can review your current commitments."

Jim clicked on his Calendar and Holly noticed is was showing the *Day* view. "Before we go any further," said Holly, "I'd like to recommend using the Week view on your Calendar. The *Day* view puts blinders on you, limiting your vision and compromising your ability to plan. But using the *Week* view will give you a really good bird's-eye view of your commitments for the whole week."

"OK," Jim nodded. "The entire week is a lot to look at, which is why I usually use the *Day* view, but I understand why the *Week* view would be more useful." He switched into Week view and waited as Holly studied his calendar.

"Now, I see you have several meetings scheduled at the same time," she commented. "You can't be in two places at once, so tell me more about these appointments."

"Some are duplicates that result when I put a meeting on my calendar and then accept an invite to the same meeting," he explained. "I can delete the duplicates, and some appointments are just reminders that two meetings are being held at the same time. Is there a better way to do this?" He looked up at Holly for advice.

"Needing to be in two places at one time is a common dilemma," Holly said, "but since that's not possible, let's make sure your calendar reflects how you actually intend to spend your time. For instance, on Friday morning, which meeting are you most likely to attend?"

Jim thought for a moment. "I'll probably make a brief appearance at the Sales meeting first, but then join the meeting with John, the owner, and Sherry, the IT Director."

"OK, then make the appointment for the Sales meeting reflect approximately how long you'll be there—maybe 9:00 to 9:15 am instead of 9:00 to 10:00 am, as you have now. Then adjust the other meeting to show that you'll spend 9:15 to 10:00 am with John and Sherry. The two meetings should appear stacked, not side by side, on your calendar."

Jim made the changes and immediately saw the difference in his calendar. "That makes a lot of sense and it's a lot less confusing."

"Yes, it is," Holly agreed. "It's important to have a calendar that's both clear and accurate, without confusion, duplicates or clutter. It should reflect *exactly* where you'll be and for how long. That is, of course, if you can adjust an appointment without affecting anyone else's calendar or the actual meeting times."

"Right," Jim agreed. "I'm not always the host or the creator of the meeting. I'm just invited."

"Yes, and that will happen, of course," Holly said, "but for the rest of your appointments, if you have a chance to be literal, I recommend it. And just like everything else you've learned so far about making progress, your calendar is best supported by ongoing decision making. Make decisions about where you really intend to be. If you're not going to join a meeting, take it off your calendar."

"Got it," Jim said as he made a few adjustments to some future appointments and deleted one he decided he simply wasn't going to attend after all.

Taskology Tip #10

It's important to have a calendar that is both clear and accurate – without confusion, duplicates or clutter – so you know exactly where you'll be and for how long.

"And one more thing, Jim," Holly added. "Do you have any tasks on your calendar?"

"Let me see…,"Jim said, as he took a closer look. "Yes. I have two calls I need to make on these two days."

"Are they *scheduled* calls?" Holly asked.

"No. I just don't want to forget to call these two people."

"Did you promise these two people you'd call them on those particular days?"

"No, but that was my plan," Jim said.

"Well, since they're not scheduled calls and you didn't promise to call these two people on those two days, they really shouldn't be on your Calendar."

"They should go on my Task List?" asked Jim.

"Yes, for two reasons: One, so you can prioritize these calls with everything else you need to do, and two, so you can save time when viewing your calendar. If someone requests to meet with you, you want to be able to see your available time very quickly, without wasting time trying to figure out which little blocks are the *real* commitments."

"OK, that makes sense," Jim said. "But what if I'm trying to decide whether or not to accept a meeting and I'm looking at my Calendar, but I forget what's on my Task List?"

"There are two things to guide you," Holly said. "The first is using the Task List as intended, knowing you have an average amount of tasks you need to do each day and that you haven't overloaded any particular day with too many tasks. The other will be better understood after our lesson today on time management. But before we get to that, take a moment to remove those two calls from your Calendar and add them to your Task List."

Jim added the calls to his Task List, complete with task descriptions and *Do Dates*.

"Great. Let's move further into time management," Holly continued. "Now that you have your Task List, you need to *protect* time in your day to actually *work* the list. Your first step is to find out how much time you've already committed. If you're overcommitted with very little flexible time, it could mean people are stealing time from you or you could be freely giving too much of it away."

"Aha," Jim said, nodding. "I know both of those are happening all the time."

"Exactly. So tell me how you manage your time today. Do you get a lot of interruptions?" asked Holly.

"Oh, yeah. Constantly."

"Define *constantly*."

"Probably a couple of times an hour. Maybe fifteen or twenty times a day."

"And how do you feel about the *open-door policy*, Jim? As a leader, how available do you feel you need to be?"

Jim thought for a few seconds. "I think having an open-door policy is good. I believe I'm here to guide my team and I need to be available to others, so I try not to shut my door unless I'm having a meeting in here. If I shut my door at other times I feel guilty about it."

"A lot of leaders say that. Tell me why you feel guilty."

"Because I don't want to disappear and have my team or my colleagues think I'm not here when they need me. I want to be a team player," Jim said. "And I like being a mentor. The visits from other people break up my day and keep things interesting."

"I'm glad you enjoy those aspects of your role, Jim, and I'm not suggesting you give them up entirely, but an *all-day, open-door policy* is costly. Do you know why?"

"Probably because the interruptions break my concentration."

"Exactly," Holly said. "Too many interruptions stop you from finishing what you start, and you lose time trying to recover from the interruptions. Sometimes, you can really lose track of where you were. Then you end up bouncing from task to task, completely forgetting that you haven't finished what you started. That's part of the *reactivity* professionals experience during the workday—all day long—and that's what we want to avoid. Reactivity is the enemy of productivity."

"Sounds familiar," he said. "The bouncing around, I mean. It happens all the time."

"Give me an example," she suggested.

"For instance, I'll finish a call with a prospect, but before I can make notes in their folder, someone walks into my office and interrupts my train of thought. As soon as they leave, I get a call from a customer and we talk for five minutes. When I get off the phone, I make notes in their file, but I still haven't made notes about the earlier phone call with the prospect. Then someone *else* walks into my office, so I focus on what *they* want. . ." Jim threw up his hands in helplessness.

"I understand," Holly said. "Studies have shown that our brains can't handle doing more than one thing at a time. Trying to do too much at once, or bouncing back and forth between tasks, is inefficient. It consumes too much time and energy."

"And I thought I was a great multitasker!" Jim said with a smile. "So what should I do instead?"

"Well, Jim," Holly began, "when you're *reactive* to the requests of others, you're not as proactive in following your own agenda. You're following someone else's agenda. You're answering the phone, you're glued to email and you're entertaining every visitor who stops by. That makes it very difficult for you to try to get something of significance accomplished with the left-over time scraps. It's true, you're a leader in this company and you're here to lead, mentor, guide, and answer questions—but not for 100% of the day. You've got to *protect* some time for yourself and there's no need to feel guilty about that. And remember this: *You get what you tolerate*, so if you continue to *invite* and *accept* interruptions, you'll continue to *receive* interruptions."

Jim nodded, listening intently. "That's good. I need to write that down. *You get what you tolerate.*"

Holly continued. "Just a minute ago you estimated how many interruptions you get during the day, but I'm guessing you didn't include phone calls or the added distractions from emails, right?"

"That's right," he answered, grimacing. "I don't suppose you can make those stop, can you?"

"Sadly, no," Holly laughed. "But I *can* help you establish and use your *Time Guard.*"

"My what?" Jim asked, raising his eyebrows.

"Your *Time Guard,*" Holly said. "It's something everyone can use. Picture an invisible force field around your office. When your door is closed, this force field is so strong that interruptions and people bounce off of it. Your force field represents the commitment you make to what you will and will not let interrupt you and your train of thought. So feel free to use your open-door policy for 80% of the day, but guard the remaining 20% of your day—or more— with a strong commitment to your priorities."

"So how many hours should I protect?" Jim asked.

"Protect at least two to three hours a day, every day, for uninterrupted

Taskology Tip #11
Protect Your Time

Maintaining an all-day, open-door policy is inefficient and costly. Block a minimum of two hours of uninterrupted time per day on your calendar so you're reminded that you need that time. You don't want others to steal it and you don't want to give it away too quickly.

time," Holly said. "You can use these hours separately or together, and you can use them for doing tasks on your Task List, processing email, or working on a special project. Get into the habit of closing your door a little more often to focus on *one* thing at a time—whatever it is—and finish what you start. Are you ready to try that?"

"Well, I've already tried closing my door, but I found that people will still knock and some will even walk in, whether I say to come in or not! It's frustrating."

"Well, you can remedy that by setting *new* expectations about what a closed door means," said Holly. "Start with your sales team and your assistant, Jennifer, and then continue sharing your plan with other colleagues and John, your boss. The next chance you get, perhaps in a department meeting, explain to your team that you're working on improving your workload management and productivity skills. Tell them why you need uninterrupted time and what it means when they see a closed door from now on. Assure them you're only unavailable for at most an hour and then you'll open your door again. If someone forgets and they walk in anyway, you can just politely remind them that you'd like to be uninterrupted, and then ask when you can get back to them."

"OK," Jim nodded. "I'll put that on the agenda for the next meeting with my sales team, early next week. I think I have a task for that!" Jim said, pleased he thought of his Task List.

"While you add that agenda item to your Task List, I'll share a little story I think you'll appreciate about people trying to walk in on a closed door. I worked with the office manager of a mortgage company several years ago and, like you, she had so many interruptions that she was having trouble concentrating and finishing her tasks. To remedy this, I suggested she shut her door every day for one hour. She selected from 10:00 to 11:00 every morning. We communicated this to the co-owners of the company, with whom I had already worked, and she set expectations with the whole office so everyone knew what to expect.

"A week later, she reported how much she loved this quiet time to get things done. Not only that, but she had discovered that one of the keys to making it work was locking her door. I loved hearing that. Apparently, there were quite a few people who didn't respect a closed door and would try to barge in any way! But locking the door solved that.

"The following week, she said she extended her quiet time to TWO hours, taking from 10:00 am until noon each day for herself. She shut her door, locked it and really enjoyed this time to become even *more* productive. She loved being able to focus on her tasks and get them accomplished, free from distractions and interruptions. And both before and after this time, she was still able to meet the needs of her team mates."

"That's so great!" Jim said, relishing the idea of locking his door. "But what if there's an urgent call or an emergency?"

"All you have to do is define what constitutes an *emergency* with your team and your assistant," said Holly. "Usually, most things can wait for an hour, but if there's a true emergency, of course you'll have to respond. You'll know what to do when the time comes. Start practicing with your team and once you see a boost in your productivity, I think you'll want to protect even *more* time for yourself with even *more* determination."

"You may be right," Jim said. "And maybe I'll tell them that *they* need to get some uninterrupted time for themselves, too."

"Yes!" Holly said. "Everyone deserves to protect some time in their day to get things done. Remember… you're unavailable every time we have our three-hour appointments, and no one interrupts you, right? And there have been no grave consequences, have there?"

"No. You're right. There haven't been," Jim said.

"Just remember this: If you continue to allow interruptions with an open-door policy, you'll risk losing time, focus, concentration, quality, speed and productivity every time."

"I agree," Jim nodded.

"Of course, there will be days when you *are* expecting an important phone call or a critical email and you'll remain open to those. But otherwise, during your time blocks, don't entertain interruptions, pick up the phone or get distracted by email unless email processing is your intended purpose for one of those time blocks. Also, you should still have available, flexible time *outside* of these protected time blocks for getting things done. You'll just have an open door during this time instead of a closed one."

"Got it," Jim said. "Should I schedule this time on my calendar now or just wing it from day to day?"

"Great question, Jim. I'll counter your question with another question. Do you think you'll have trouble *protecting* two hours a day if you *don't* schedule it now?"

Jim thought for a moment as he looked at his calendar on the screen. "Yes. Others will see how much time I have available and they'll schedule appointments and invite me to meetings. But if I block that time, no one will take it!"

"Exactly," Holly said. "I recommend protecting at least an hour in the morning and an hour in the afternoon."

"Should those be at the same time every day?" Jim asked.

"No, they don't have to be. You'll start out that way as we target your best times of day to protect and set them up on a recurring basis, but going forward from week to week you'll move each one around to accommodate other meetings and calls. But here's the rule." Holly paused. "You can move these blocks around, but *try not to delete them.* OK?"

"OK, got it. I think I'll protect from 9:00 to 10:00 every morning and then from 2:00 to 3:00 every afternoon." He took the mouse and started to set up the first appointment, then stopped. "What do I call this time?"

"Use a general name like *Office Time* or *Do Not Schedule/DNS* or *Quiet Time.* Just don't call it anything too specific. Leave it vague. You'll decide from day to day how you want to use it."

Jim set up two recurring appointments, one in the morning and one in the afternoon, every weekday, with no end date to the recurrence. Then Holly instructed him to look at the next three weeks and move his new time blocks around to accommodate existing appointments and calls. "Remember to keep an eye out for conflicts with other scheduled commitments. You don't want to see side-by-side appointments. Everything should be stacked, so shift your time blocks around accordingly."

"There," Jim said when he was finished. "I have protected time!" He felt better already, just knowing that he had preserved time to make progress on things he needed to do.

"Great!" Holly said. "Going forward, I want you to notice how you use your time blocks. It's unrealistic to expect you'll be able to preserve *every* one of them, but keep and use as many as possible. Otherwise, you'll miss out on this time to get things done. And that means you're tossing the plan right out the window, so be careful. This time is for you. I want you to have it because I know you need it."

"I do!" Jim said emphatically. "I'll talk with my team and Jennifer and others about these time blocks and explain why I'll be closing my door a bit more often."

"Good!" Holly said. "And remind your team that you're not disappearing for hours on end. It's just an hour and they can most likely hold their questions until you're available again. And remember to define *emergencies* and *urgent situations* for them so you're all on the same page and they know what to do."

Now, let's switch gears and talk more about your Task List," Holly continued. "This morning when I arrived, you mentioned you're keeping an eye on how many tasks you actually get done. About how many tasks are you getting accomplished every day, on average?"

Jim looked at his Task List, thinking back over the past week. "About five or six. I was planning seven, eight or nine tasks on a couple of days, but I ended up having to move some forward to another day. I just didn't have as much time as I thought."

Holly smiled. "Well, when you plan and prioritize it will really help to look at your Calendar *first,* so you're aware of which days are good for accomplishing tasks. At a glance, you want to be able to assess how many tasks you can target for each day and avoid planning tasks for days when you're at too many meetings or out at an all-day conference. Get into the habit of checking your Calendar whenever you're adding new tasks to your Task List or reprioritizing so you keep your plan realistic."

"Got it," said Jim, nodding slowly. "Then I can see what I realistically have time for. On some days I might be able to do seven and other days only three or four."

"Exactly. This should be a *will-do* list, not a *wish list*. If the list is unrealistic, it won't support you or your productivity. And now that we've talked about using the *Week view* and you've removed tasks that don't belong, you'll see a more accurate reflection of your available time each week.

"And remember when you asked me earlier about accepting appointments with others when you don't remember what's on your Task List?" Jim nodded. "I said you'll have two things to guide you. One, you already know to plan doing an average of five or six tasks each day and you'll be careful not to overload any day with too many tasks. The second thing you now have guiding you is the protected time on your calendar for working on those tasks."

"Now I'll know that I've got time reserved on my calendar for working on tasks," Jim said, catching on. "And I can do a better job of matching up the number of tasks I plan to do with the available time I have each day."

"Right," Holly said. "You have to make sure you have enough time each day to accomplish the tasks you said you wanted to do. You can even expand your time blocks and protect even more time on certain days to make sure you get the time you need."

"It'll be a lot easier to look at my calendar and see in an instant what's available and what's not," Jim continued.

"And you'll have peace of mind knowing that you've protected time for accomplishing important tasks. Keep a strong task-time connection and you'll never back yourself into a corner with too little time for getting things done."

"I like it," Jim said, understanding more clearly the task-time connection.

"Now, let's practice," Holly continued. "Look at today and tomorrow on your Calendar and then look at your Task List. What do you think about the number of tasks listed for today and tomorrow, given the types of tasks they are and the time you have available?"

Jim clicked on his calendar and assessed his open, flexible time as well as the number of meetings and calls he had scheduled. Then he clicked on his Task List and saw eight tasks planned for today and nine listed for tomorrow. He hesitated to move anything, so Holly started by asking him how much time each task would require. Jim identified a few five-minute tasks and a few that would require twenty or thirty minutes. When he realized which tasks he should move to future dates, he started reprioritizing his list.

"There," he said one minute later. "Done. Should I look at next week's tasks, too?"

"Yes. When you check your Calendar first, you'll remember to keep your Task List realistic. I'd rather you be a rock star and get your top priorities accomplished and feel really good about that, instead of feeling frustrated every day because you're trying to do too much, you know?"

"I do know—first hand, in fact," Jim said. "Last week I tried to do too much, and I was frustrated when I couldn't accomplish everything. And I still had a lot of interruptions every day, which didn't help."

"Yes, let's talk about those interruptions," Holly said. "Do any of your team members interrupt you more than others? Or are you working closely with anyone right now on certain projects?"

"It's not a project, but Aimee is one of our new sales directors and she visits me a lot. She's still learning the ropes. Why?"

"Because sometimes, even when you're using your time blocks, you could still be interrupted A LOT during the *rest* of your day by visitors like Aimee," Holly answered. "A new team member asking questions and getting guidance is certainly a good thing, but I recommend you *channel* these interruptions instead of fielding them all day long.

"What do you mean by *channeling?*"

"Channeling is a way for you to *pull* interruptions into a specific time frame that works for both of you rather than allowing people to *push* them at you all day long. You can channel information and questions into brief, one-to-one meetings. Since Aimee visits you a lot, perhaps you could schedule a 10-minute meeting with her every morning or afternoon, and ask her to collect her questions and hold them until you meet. Unless a question is truly urgent, you can tell Aimee and the rest of your team to hold questions so they don't visit you every… single… time… something… comes up. That way, you can reduce the interruptions and still give people time to ask questions, and *all* of you will have more time for yourselves. You can stay focused for longer periods of time so you can get things done and make more progress. How does that sound?"

"It sounds like a great solution. I'll give it a try," said Jim. "I don't know if 10 minutes is enough time, but I'll find out once Aimee and I start meeting. I enjoy the interactions, but sometimes I do get tired of the interruptions. Some days, I feel like I'm at the mercy of everyone else."

"Well, now you have a few new strategies to protect your time. And when you plan your tasks realistically and use your time blocks, you can get your priorities accomplished and still be there for your team."

"Fantastic!" Jim said, happy to have a new perspective on his time.

"OK, Jim, it's almost time to wrap up these lessons on time management. You've done a great job! You've got an incredibly powerful Task List and newly protected time blocks. How are you feeling about your progress so far?"

"Wonderful! I can't believe how much has changed in just one week. I really know what's going on now. I know when I'm getting stuck or when I'm letting things stall or when I'm moving too fast to make decisions. I know enough now to avoid falling into these traps when I see them."

Jim felt really good about his progress. Being in a clutter-free office was a great feeling—a great reminder for him the next time he was tempted to hold onto something *just in case*. He would also remember to stop and think when he was tempted to put something down somewhere because he didn't know what to do with it or because he was too rushed to review it.

"I'm going to save *so much time* not managing so much *stuff* anymore. I have a place for all my tasks now, which is great, and now I'll have a better handle on my time. So email is next, right?" Jim asked.

"We'll get there soon!" Holly said. "We're going to address files next—both paper and digital—and *then* we'll get into your email. In preparation for these upcoming phases, I encourage you to connect with a legal authority in the company about the Records Retention Guidelines. It's important that you understand what to keep, both physically and electronically—where to keep documents and how long you're required to keep them."

She explained to Jim that different clients were required to keep different types of paper files or digital documents according to their industry. And some clients were required to save ALL emails in the email system, while others had different guidelines for saving, archiving, and deleting emails and attachments. "I'd like you to be clear on the specific guidelines for Octagon Office Solutions so you can move quickly and confidently in making decisions about paper, files, electronic documents and emails in our coming appointments."

"Sure, I'll find out what our policy is," said Jim. "In fact, I'll add that to my Task List right now!"

Holly laughed. "What a great idea! Now, I'll let you get back to your day and I'll see you next week." She stood and gathered her things, and Jim walked her out to the lobby.

Back in his office, Jim sat down at his computer, clicked on his email and groaned when he saw his Inbox was overflowing with new email. *The flood never stops,* he thought to himself. *I can't wait to get to the email lessons with Holly.*

Chapter 12 Summary

- **Maintain a calendar that's both clear and accurate**, without confusion, duplicates or clutter, so you know exactly where you'll be each day and for how long.

- **Use the *Week* or *Month* view for viewing your calendar.** The Day view puts blinders on you, limiting your ability to see what's coming up and compromising your ability to plan.

- **Maintaining an all-day, open-door policy is inefficient and costly.** When you allow interruptions without limitation, you're more likely to react to the requests of others instead of being proactive with your own agenda. An open-door policy risks the loss of time, focus, concentration, quality, speed and productivity.

- **Use your *Time Guard* and close your door** for periods of time so you can focus without interruption to get things done. An all-day, open-door policy is fine for 80% of the day, but guard the remaining 20% of your day with a strong commitment to your priorities. Guard this time so others won't steal it and you won't give it away so readily.

- **Protect at least two hours a day**, every day, for uninterrupted time. Schedule these hours separately or together, for doing tasks on your Task List, processing email, or working on special projects.

- **A calendar is for scheduled appointments and commitments.** The Task List is for tasks. Avoid putting tasks on a calendar unless the task will take at least 45-60 minutes or more to do.

- **Look at your calendar first** before adding or reprioritizing tasks so you're aware of the days that are best for accomplishing tasks as well as how many tasks to plan for certain days.

- **"Channeling" is a way to *pull* interruptions into a specific time frame** that works for you rather than to allowing people to *push* them at you all day long. Channel information and questions from others into brief, one-to-one meetings so you can all enjoy fewer interruptions and more focus during the day.

CHAPTER 13

Getting Organized

IN THE APPOINTMENTS to follow, Holly worked with Jim to organize both his physical office files, plus his electronic files in the hard drive.

"Let's start with your physical files," said Holly. "As you created your Task List, you found and set aside these papers and files you'd like to keep for future reference," Holly said as she rested her hand on top of the pile, "and today we're going to put them away in new files. But first, we need to see what's in these two credenza drawers and this one desk drawer."

"I really haven't looked in my credenza drawers much in the past year, since I mostly use the drawer in my desk," said Jim. "But the last time I looked for something in my credenza, the files were so overstuffed I could hardly pull something out, much less put something in."

When he and Holly began investigating, they discovered that the drawers in the credenza were mostly full of outdated files. Holly suggested they start there.

Jim felt a bit overwhelmed as he looked at the first drawer. He had no idea where to start and was grateful for Holly's guidance. She taught him how to make decisions about paper and information so he'd better understand what to keep and what to toss while still following the company's records retention policy he had identified and shared with Holly.

"I usually just keep everything, whether or not I really need it," Jim said, grimacing at the drawer they were working on. "I'm always worried I might need something again in the future."

"If you need to replace only one or two things out of every one hundred things you let go of, it will be worth your time to recover them, and you'll enjoy being free of the other ninety-eight things," said Holly. "Remember that the less you keep, the less you have to manage, and the more time you'll save when you're looking for important papers and files in the future. You shouldn't have to sift through old, outdated or useless information to find what you need."

"I totally agree," Jim said. "I look forward to using my time on more important priorities than shuffling papers around or searching for things. I'm tired of wasting time."

Taskology Tip #12

The less you keep, the less you have to manage and the more time you'll save for yourself.

Jim and Holly worked together until they had emptied the drawers in his credenza and created a new system for the papers and files he wanted to keep. Once those drawers were finished, they turned their attention to the desk drawer, using the same process to create new files for the things he especially wanted to keep at his fingertips.

When they were finished, Jim looked at his new file drawers which were now fully organized and categorized. "Wow, this is amazing," he said, pulling out each file drawer, one by one. "I feel like a great weight has been lifted from my shoulders. Now I know I'll be able to quickly find or file any document I need."

"Exactly right, Jim. Now you can easily file away what you want to keep, instead of cluttering up your desk with reference papers and files. They don't need to be *out* anymore, especially if you're not currently using them to accomplish a task or a project. And now that we have your physical files organized, let's shift gears and talk about how to organize and manage electronic documents in your computer."

"I'm relieved we're tackling this," said Jim. "I never took the time to figure out the best way to set up a system for my documents, so I mostly use my desktop for anything I really need."

"A lot of people do that, too. How's it working for you as a system?" asked Holly.

"Well, the short answer is that it's not working," he said. "There's no order to the files on my computer desktop, so I still waste time searching for what I need, and sometimes I never find it! It's really frustrating."

Holly and Jim created a new system for his electronic documents and folders in his computer, including every document and file that was showing on his desktop. First, they reviewed a random list of documents they found in the C: drive, which was merely a long list of several hundred documents in alphabetical order and with no rhyme or reason. Then they reviewed the few dozen documents and folders on his desktop—a haphazard array of icons completely covering his screen.

During the review process, Jim learned how to set up new folders, categorize his documents, and rename documents for easy retrieval. One of the most important lessons he learned was how to name files more accurately and descriptively.

"The trick is to never have to open a document to see what it is," Holly explained. "Your document names shouldn't create mystery. These documents should be so well-named that you know exactly what they are without having to open them."

"And I had to open the bulk of them today," Jim laughed.

"Right," Holly agreed. "So always start with a noun—with *what it is*—and then use adjectives, dates, etc... Use as many descriptive words as you need so you know what the document is."

When they were finished, Jim had cleared his computer desktop and deleted a lot of old documents and folders he no longer needed. Going forward, he knew he had a cohesive system he could rely on for all of his electronic documents—and he thoroughly understood the system because he'd helped build it.

"I can finally save a document in my computer in an actual system. I know where to put it and I know I can find it again fast without running a Search," said Jim. "And I'm thrilled that I can reduce the amount of paper I need to keep and use my electronic document library instead. Jim was looking forward to having less stress and saving more time, now that he didn't have to search for anything... anywhere... anymore.

The only remaining icons on Jim's desktop represented shortcuts to the programs and applications he used every day. And finally, Jim could see the photo on his computer desktop of his family at the beach last summer. The photo brought back some great memories and made him realize his desktop could now be a great source of peace rather than stress and confusion.

During the final lesson on file management, Jim mentioned that Octagon Office Solutions was shopping for a cloud-based document management system. Holly assured him that the system she'd taught him for organizing electronic documents could be used anywhere, whether on a server or in the cloud. But, she explained, no matter where electronic documents are stored, they still need to be organized and categorized in a structure that's simple, logical and easy to use for finding and filing documents quickly.

"Jim, now that both your physical files and your electronic document library are set up, I think you're ready for the next set of lessons," said Holly.

"Is it *finally* time for email?" asked Jim.

"Yes, it's *finally* time," Holly said, laughing as Jim gave two thumbs up. "The lessons will include a review of your email folders first and then we'll work in your Inbox. We'll get started the next time we meet."

CHAPTER 14

Simplifying Email Folders

THE DAY BEFORE their next appointment, Holly called Jim to switch their onsite appointment to a phone call and a computer interface instead. An early snowstorm had begun that morning and heavy snow accumulation was expected overnight. Jim agreed that working virtually would be an effective way to continue making progress despite the weather.

Unfortunately for Jim, he still had to drive to work on Wednesday morning, but as he slowly made his way in, he realized he was looking forward to the upcoming call with Holly. Today, he'd begin his journey to email mastery and finally take control of his Inbox. He could stop wasting time looking for emails and attachments, stop losing track of to-dos and follow-ups, and put an end to the constant reactivity caused by incoming email.

Shortly after arriving at the office, Jim called Holly promptly at 9:00 am as he started to thaw out with his first cup of hot coffee.

"I'm glad we could still have our appointment, despite the weather," Jim said after they exchanged greetings. "I can't *wait* to get a grip on my email."

"I'm sure! This is going to be a big day for you," Holly said. "But before we get started on email, tell me how it's going with your Task List and everything else we've worked on until now."

As their computers connected and interfaced, Jim summarized for Holly all the different ways he was making progress. He was enjoying the Task List and the clarity it provided, and was relying on it to guide him. He was also taking advantage of his new time blocks, which gave him an average of two hours of uninterrupted time each day. By honoring his time blocks, he'd been able to focus on his work for longer periods of time and complete tasks from start to finish. His assistant Jennifer had also become an important ally, fiercely protecting his time and refusing to give away his time blocks. Only Jim could give away a time block, if push came to shove, and so far he'd only let go of one or two.

"That's great, Jim. It's always nice when someone like Jennifer becomes an ally in defending and protecting your time," said Holly.

Jim added that he'd shared his goals with his colleagues and his boss, and everyone was supportive. "I've also let my direct reports know that I'm not to be interrupted when my door is closed, unless it's an emergency—and I've defined what that means. I've also told them to collect their questions before coming to see me, and to come prepared with potential solutions. And as you suggested, I set up short, regular meetings with Aimee, the new sales director, so I can address all of her questions at once."

"You've really taken your performance to a higher level, Jim," said Holly. "Congratulations! You're working the system and following through on all kinds of solutions. And you seem happier and much less stressed."

"I am," Jim said. "I feel like I have more control of my day. By using this Task List I've got a clear picture of what I need to do and when, and even if my day gets thrown off, I'm not completely sidetracked. I simply adjust and keep going, without missing or forgetting anything.

"I'm also apologizing a lot less to others for not following up, not calling back, not emailing, or for losing track of information. As a matter of fact," he said with pride, "just yesterday, the president of the company asked me about two big lease renewals, and I had the information right at my fingertips."

"Way to go!" Holly said. "That sounds very different from the scenario that might have unfolded a couple months ago, right?"

"Totally," Jim agreed. "Looking back, I realize now how disorganized I really was."

Jim was pleased with the progress he'd made in just a month, and he felt confident that more progress was still to come. With Holly's guidance, he was finally becoming the leader at Octagon he'd intended to be. And with what he was learning from Taskology, he knew he could increase his sales faster, with more attention to detail, and work more often with his sales team to help them grow—without working longer hours or adding to his stress.

"How are you doing with your files and your electronic document library?"

Jim smiled. "I can finally find what I need in both – and *fast*! I'm saving so much time. It's awesome! And I've also saved a lot of attachments from email, confident I won't lose them in the hard drive or on my desktop."

"That's great, Jim! And we're just getting into email today, so this is a perfect segue into the next set of lessons. You'll continue to see the benefits of Taskology as you apply what you learn about email management."

"Sounds great. Where do we start?"

"We'll start by establishing a reliable system of email folders, just like we set up reliable systems for your Task List, your Calendar and your files. After we address your email folders, we'll finally get into the Inbox.

As Jim and Holly were connected through the computer interface, Holly could already see Jim's email screen. "Well, you have a long list of email folders," Holly said after a few moments. "I'm guessing there are at least forty or fifty folders here, plus it looks like you have sub-folders in many of them."

Holly had seen lists like this before, of course, and knew right away that Jim had probably saved too much and set up too many folders in the process, just like many other professionals who believe *more folders = greater organization*. But there's such a thing as *over-organizing* and she believed Jim had done just that.

"I guess I thought that creating folders was the only way I could keep track of everything," Jim said. "But I've since identified our Records Retention Guidelines for email and I found out that I don't need to keep as much as I thought I did."

"That's good to know, Jim. Knowing the guidelines up front will help you make decisions today and every day forward about your email. And I'm glad you're ready and able to part with some of your emails. When you have this many folders, you're losing time scrolling and searching through the list to find things and also when you want to file something from your Inbox. Again, when you're looking for emails later, the time you spend searching adds up.

"Also, it looks like a lot of your folders are named for the people who sent you emails, plus a variety of other topics. When this kind of structure exists, it becomes burdensome and counter-productive to navigate the list."

Jim nodded in agreement. "It does take a while to find what I'm looking for," he said with exasperation, ready to learn a better way.

"There are three goals to achieve when taking control of your email so you can manage it more efficiently and effectively. When these goals are accomplished, you can save a lot of time and energy. They are ORGANIZE, CENTRALIZE and MINIMIZE.

"To ORGANIZE means streamlining your folders list. We're going to consolidate folders that share a similar topic and put them into fewer, but broader Major Category folders. This will shorten your folder list, which will make navigation faster and easier for you and that will save you time."

"Having less to scroll through sounds great," Jim said.

"We'll also CENTRALIZE information that belongs elsewhere in other systems for reference or action," Holly explained. "This means we'll decide where the information belongs and move it to that location. In some cases, we'll save contact information into Contacts or add event or meeting information to your Calendar or save attachments in your e-document library. In other cases, you'll add tasks to your Task List or maybe print something and file it in a physical file."

And the third one, MINIMIZE, means we'll reduce the number of emails and folders you keep overall. You should keep only what's useful to you—or what's required by your records retention guidelines—and archive or delete the rest."

"Sounds good," Jim nodded. "So, how do we start?"

"First, you'll make one major structural change to your folder list, because I see that your folders are mixed in with system folders. Let's create two new main folders—one called *Business* and the other *Personal*—and make these sub-folders of the Inbox."

Jim hesitated. "OK, and why am I doing that?"

"Creating these two folders will allow us to separate business emails from personal emails and consolidate each category into two main folders. And making these sub-folders of the Inbox separates them from your system folders, like *Deleted*, *Drafts*, *Junk*, *Outbox* and *Sent*. You want to be able to zero in on your folders and not have to sift through a list that includes system folders you don't need to see."

"OK. That makes sense," Jim said. "Can I call my *Business* folder *Octagon* instead?"

"Certainly!" she answered. "And within these two main folders for *Octagon* and *Personal*, you'll have what I call Major Category folders. This list of folders should be as short as possible so the whole list is completely visible on one screen without scrolling." Holly added that they'd spend today's time on his *Octagon* folders only, and recommended that Jim review his personal emails as homework. She instructed him to consolidate all of his personal folders in the list and move them into the new main folder called *Personal*.

"Everything you review today will go into a Major Category folder," continued Holly, "or into a sub-folder that further categorizes the data in a Major Category folder. You already have a lot of folders, so some may become Major Category folders and others will become sub-folders. You may also create new folders in the process, too. I'll show you what I mean as we begin our review." She added that once Jim had reviewed email folders he decided to keep, he should move them immediately to the new *Octagon* folder as a Major Category folder or as a subfolder. All other email folders would stay put until he reviewed them, so it would be easy to know which folders had been reviewed and organized and which had not.

"Holly, can you give me some examples of Major Category folders?"

"Sure. Major Category folders are used for things like projects, products, services, programs, jobs, or departments. Common examples of Major Category folders are Finance, Admin, Marketing, Training, Vendors, and Clients, but we'll set up folders that are specific to you and your position here at Octagon. I'll guide you through the whole process. You'll end up with a short but useful list of Major Category folders."

"Should I set up my category folders now? The ones I know I'll need?" Jim asked.

"Not yet, Jim," said Holly. "Like I said, you probably already have some folders you'll need in your list, but never spend time up front trying to anticipate what you'll need because you could waste your time. Many of my clients have done that in the past, and then when we met and started working together, they ended up deleting folders they didn't need after all. You first have to figure out what kinds of emails you're keeping, and then—and *only then*—will you need a folder or sub-folder to contain what you're keeping."

"Got it." Jim said. "So, should I start the review now?"

"I want clarify one thing before we begin," Holly said quickly. "As we work on your email folders today, the *organizing, centralizing* and *minimizing* will occur all at the same time. You'll move folders around, delete emails, consolidate folders and create new folders as necessary, so expect these steps to overlap as you go through the review process."

"Good to know," Jim said as he opened the first folder at the top of the list and started his review. As he looked at the emails in each folder, Holly asked Jim to describe what the folder was for, what kinds of emails were in each folder, and how the emails were useful to him.

Holly and Jim carried on their conversations about the various folders and emails as Jim continued his review, deleting email after email. Several times he repeated quietly, "Why did I keep this?" It was a rhetorical question that needed no answer as he looked through the new lens of Holly's standard question: *How is this useful to you?* Through this process Jim was discovering that much of what he'd saved wasn't very useful at all and as a result he was deleting a lot.

"And I shouldn't keep these folders named for the people who sent me emails?" Jim asked, fairly certain of how Holly would answer.

"Correct," Holly said. "Most of those will go away, but we'll make sure any information you do need to keep is saved somewhere else. What we'll do today is centralize your emails around a topic or category. We'll name folders according to how the emails are *useful* to you and what they're for—such as projects, programs, clients or vendors— instead of naming them for who or where the emails came from. However, there may be one or two exceptions to that, which we'll address as we review your emails in both the email folders and the Inbox."

As Jim consolidated his emails and folders, he could see the benefits of keeping emails together according to a certain topic or initiative. Holly worked with Jim to help him create a more streamlined and efficient folder structure, saving other necessary information elsewhere and deleting the rest.

At one point, Holly realized Jim had quite a few folders throughout his list for both vendors and clients, and she suggested he set up two new Major

Category folders under *Octagon* — one for *Customers* and one for *Vendors*. This allowed Jim to consolidate more than a dozen folders into each category and shorten his folder list considerably.

Another opportunity for consolidation appeared when Jim saw he had a folder for each member of the *Quality Improvement Team* at Octagon. As he and Holly discussed the types of emails in each member's folder he realized he'd benefit from consolidating all of these emails in one *QI Team* folder.

Holly also recommended that Jim set up a new folder called *Travel*

Taskology Tip #13

Your email folders list should be short and visible on one screen. The structure begins with two main folders —"Business" and "Personal"—as sub-folders of the Inbox. Major Category folders within "Business" and "Personal" are named for broad categories such as projects, programs, jobs, clients, vendors or departments. Sub-folders may or may not be necessary to further sub-categorize emails within Major Category folders.

that would contain emails related to his travel plans, including reservations, accommodations, flight information, frequent flyer miles, memberships, and more. She instructed him to review this folder after each trip was over and clear out the emails he no longer needed.

When Jim found emails he'd saved solely for contact information, Holly recommended adding this information to his Contact system and deleting the email. He also saved necessary attachments in his newly organized electronic document library, now without fear of losing them. Plus, Holly showed him the many ways he could save individual attachments from an email, as well as how to save *all* attachments at once.

Along the way, Jim found conversations, company communications, policy revisions, and email messages that would be useful to reference in the future. One email he found would be particularly helpful for performance evaluations of his direct reports.

"Holly, can I save an actual email in my hard drive?" he asked. "I want to keep this message in a folder I set up for the same topic."

"Sure," she answered and showed him how to save the email in his electronic document library. Jim knew he'd use this process again to save messages he didn't want to lose track of, but didn't need to keep them in his email system. Plus, in the future, he could find emails saved in a certain folder in his e-document library without conducting a search in his e-mail system, which would save him considerable amounts of time.

Holly and Jim continued their discussions as Jim reviewed more folders, deciding what was useful and what was not. He was swiftly moving emails around, centralizing information in other locations, and deleting a lot of emails he didn't need anymore.

"You're on a roll, Jim!" Holly said.

"I'm so *done* with all these emails," Jim exclaimed. "It's like I've been given permission to let things go. Finally! I had NO idea where to put all of these emails, so I just created a ton of folders. But now I see I don't need them anymore."

Soon Jim reached a folder called *Miscellaneous/Hold.*

"Oh, this is one of my favorites," Holly said. "I've seen many folders like this, including some named *General* or *This and That,* all of which are completely taboo in the Taskology system. As you've probably already guessed, you'll have to part with this folder after saving useful information elsewhere and deleting the rest. Go ahead and click on this folder and let's see what's in there."

Jim hesitated. "I really don't want to show you what's in here... I'm sort of embarrassed about everything I've saved..."

"Go ahead, Jim," Holly said. "No matter what's in there, we need to address it. It's OK. We'll get through it."

Jim double-clicked on the folder to reveal a list of more than twenty folders. He heard Holly gasp.

He laughed at Holly's reaction. He now realized it was silly that he'd held on to *this* many emails without making decisions on *any* of them.

"OK," Holly said. "It's more than I expected, but let's see what you have here."

Sifting through the subfolders and emails in the *Miscellaneous/Hold* folder, Jim realized that most dated back to his first year at Octagon and were obsolete.

Some folders had been created because he was waiting on something or someone, but since it was way past the time of action, he no longer needed those either.

A few other subfolders held emails that Jim had saved simply because he didn't know what to do with them. At some point, Holly explained, all of these emails belonged in other locations for reference or action, but since most were no longer needed, he'd save only the most important emails in different folders and any other kinds of information he was sure to reference in the future. The rest he would delete.

After Jim finished his review of the *Miscellaneous/Hold* folder, he breathed a deep sigh of relief. "I can't believe it, but I'm finished with this huge folder, never to be used again."

"It was quite a collection," Holly said, "but look at how much you *didn't* need any more."

"You're right," Jim laughed. "After conquering that folder, I feel like anything is possible!"

Following the review of several more folders, Jim clicked on a folder called *Reading*.

"What about this one?" Holly asked. "It looks like you've accumulated quite a bit of reading."

"Yeah… I just never seem to get around to all the stuff I save to read," Jim said. "I had a few *Rules* set up to automatically put emails in here so I could get them out of my Inbox, but then I never actually read them."

"I'll come back to using *Rules* in just a minute, Jim, but first let's talk about reading. It's one of the more challenging areas for most clients, both from a processing standpoint and because of the time needed to read. Remember when we talked about one of my Quick Start Guides, *Reach for the S.T.A.R.R.s?* The second *R* in S.T.A.R.R. is for reading. In that lesson we discussed that if you're just accumulating information without reading it, you're not gaining any value from it. We need to follow that same principle with reading you set aside in email. So, with email in mind, let's cover this again.

"First, if you have trouble keeping up with what you really want to read, you need to protect time to read. Without time, you'll never do it. Second, you really must read everything you saved to read by the end of the week. Do you remember why?" she asked.

"Yep," said Jim. "Because more reading is already on its way."

"Exactly," Holly said. "I hope that will prevent you from collecting too much reading in the future."

"It's true. I collect things I want to read, but I then don't have time to read them," he said.

"You have time to read, Jim," Holly said with a smile, "*if* you make reading a priority… and you protect the time to do it. Now, let's take a look at what you've saved and see if any of it is still useful to you."

Jim scrolled through the contents of his *Reading* folder. Within a couple minutes he had deleted all but two emails, which involved more current material. He decided to add one of the emails to his Task List since it was critical reading that would likely produce a follow-up step he didn't want to forget.

"Great job, Jim!" Holly said. "That kind of decisiveness is common when reviewing old reading materials. Much of what gets put aside ages quickly, and most clients say they'd prefer to start fresh with a new reading strategy for the future, rather than worry about reading material that's past its prime."

"I agree. I'll just start fresh. Now, what do I do with this last email in my *Reading* folder?" Jim asked.

"The same thing I recommend for all of the *new* reading that you'll get in the future: *Leave it in your Inbox*—especially if it's simple reading," she replied. "But there are a few steps I want to cover so you're clear on the process.

"First, do a cursory review to see if it's worth your time to read, which you've already done for this one, so you know you want to keep it. But for all future reading, remember the *Slow Down to Speed Up* lesson we covered in our first session together. Slow down long enough to look at what you've received and determine if it's useful. You may be able to read it within two minutes or it may not be worth your time, so you'll just delete it. If you can't read it in a minute or two, but you believe it to be worthwhile, then leave it in the Inbox and read it by the end of the day. At the latest, read it by the end of the week. And if you have trouble getting time to read, block time on your calendar for daily or weekly reading."

"And if it's *Review and Do* kind of reading I'll put it on my Task List, right?" Jim asked.

"Yes. And no matter how you remember to read or where you put the email, be sure to read what you've collected by the end of the week, because...?" Holly stopped short and looked at Jim for the answer to the pop quiz.

"More is already on its way," said Jim, grinning as he finished the sentence for Holly. "So you're saying I can't keep my *Reading* folder?"

"No, you don't need a *Reading* folder," Holly said, "but I have other clients who use one because they're disciplined about keeping up with it. I recommend only using a *Reading* folder when you *honor* the time you've blocked out for reading and you *empty* the folder every week. If you don't have that habit in place I suggest you keep reading in your Inbox."

"But then it will just add to the clutter in my Inbox," Jim said.

"Not necessarily," Holly replied. "When your Inbox is empty—and it will be soon—you'll more clearly see what you're saving to read, which may only be a couple of emails. Keeping your Inbox at or near zero will help you quickly decide what to read and what to let go of. You'll be more apt to keep up with reading and let it go, as opposed to filing it away in a folder—or using *Rules* to do it—where you can easily lose track of what you're keeping. It's too easy to accumulate more reading than you have time to read. But when *Reading* is in your Inbox, you can knock out some of it whenever you have a few minutes. Read it or delete it as soon as possible, and if it's *really* useful, you might save it elsewhere in your files or e-files for future reference."

"OK, I understand. I'll delete my *Reading* folder," said Jim. "And I might need to unsubscribe from a few things, too."

"That sounds good, on both counts," Holly said. "Now, do you want to protect time on your calendar to read each week, or do you think you'll be able to create a new habit of reading regularly each week *without* time blocks? I've seen both approaches, so you decide what works best for you."

"I don't think I need time blocks," Jim said. "But first I'll get a clearer picture of all the things I receive that I could read. Once I unsubscribe from a bunch of publications and blogs, and separate the junk from the good stuff, then I'll see what I really want to read."

"Sounds good. What's your best time of day to read? Morning or afternoon? And do you like to read at work or at home?" Holly asked.

"At work. And my best times would either be in the morning with my first cup of coffee or around lunchtime, when I sometimes eat at my desk."

"OK, great. Then you've targeted two times, initially, that are a good time to read. But if you find you're having trouble getting time to read, put a half-hour or a one-hour appointment on your calendar for yourself and *read,*" Holly said. "Deal?"

"Deal!" Jim agreed.

"Now, I touched briefly on *Rules* earlier, and I want to return to that subject for just a minute," Holly said. "You may have noticed that using *Rules* allows you to move emails around, but you're not necessarily addressing them in a timely manner. You can lose track of the volume coming in because you never see the emails in your Inbox."

"Right," Jim agreed. "That's why I had so much in my *Reading* folder—and so many emails in a few other folders that were connected to *Rules.*"

Holly nodded affirmatively and continued. "And when you have no idea what's accumulating in your folders, you won't be aware of the time you need to read your emails, process information, and plan tasks. This is how people lose the connection between volume and time—similar to the *task-time connection* for getting things done.

"Many of my clients have used *Rules* in the past for anything and everything, but they ended up regretting it because they lost track of their emails. They missed deadlines, lost track of data, forgot follow ups, and when we addressed these issues, they decided to delete *all* of their Rules and take back control of their email. So please review your *Rules* as homework and let me know what you do with them the next time we talk. I hope you'll delete all of them, but if you decide to keep any, I'd like to know which ones you're keeping and why."

"OK, I'll take a look," Jim agreed. "I may delete them all, but it's been so long since I set them up, I've forgotten what I have."

By the end of their call, Jim had reviewed almost all of what he'd accumulated in his email folders. Holly said he could review the few remaining folders as homework in the coming week, but asked him to skip a folder he'd created called *Action*, which they would address in their next session when they worked on his Inbox.

"Wow, I deleted A LOT!" Jim said. "I used to have so many folders. Look at how much we've consolidated!"

"You did a great job! You have a much shorter list now. You've got your two main folders—*Octagon* and *Personal*— which are subfolders under the Inbox and they're separate from all of the other system folders like *Junk, Sent* and *Deleted.* Then within *Octagon* you have a shorter list of Major Category folders and subfolders within those. You should be able to get around *much* faster now and look! No more scrolling!" Holly cheered as Jim expanded the folder list for *Octagon*, and it didn't go past the bottom of the screen.

"I can't believe it," Jim said quietly. "Amazing. This'll take some getting used to, but I love it already."

Chapter 14 Summary

- **ORGANIZE, CENTRALIZE and MINIMIZE**
  These are 3 main goals to achieve when taking control of email folders in order to manage reference emails more efficiently and effectively. When these goals are accomplished, you can save a lot of time and energy.
  - o **ORGANIZE** email folders that share a similar topic into fewer, but broader Major Category folders. This will consolidate folders and shorten your list. With fewer folders, navigation will be faster and easier, which will save time.
  - o **CENTRALIZE** information that belongs elsewhere in other systems for reference or action. Examples include saving contact information into Contacts, adding event or meeting information to the Calendar, saving attachments in your e-document library, and adding tasks to the Task List.
  - o **MINIMIZE** the number of emails and email folders you keep. Keep only what's useful to you or what's required by your records retention guidelines, and archive or delete the rest.
- **An email folders list should be short and visible on one screen.**
  The structure begins with two main folders—*Business* and *Personal*—as sub-folders to the Inbox. Within "Business" and "Personal" are Major Category folders, and within those are sub-folders to further categorize your email. Sub-folders may or may not be necessary for some Major Category folders.
- **Name folders according to how emails are useful to you and what they're for** instead of naming them for who or where the emails came from. Examples include projects, programs, locations, departments, vendors, customers, clients, jobs or other large categories. There are exceptions, of course, such as naming folders for those to whom you delegate tasks regularly. Otherwise, folders should NOT be named for the people who send you emails.

- **Using *Rules* has the potential to hurt your productivity.** You can lose track of the volume of emails coming in—because you never see them in your Inbox—and as a result you may never know what kind of time you need to read or review these emails, process information or plan tasks. *Rules* can prevent you from addressing emails in a timely manner, which can cause you to miss deadlines, lose track of data, and forget follow-ups.

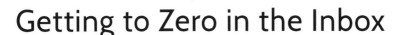

Getting to Zero in the Inbox

JIM LOOKED UP from his desk as Georgia Gansworth, director of marketing, walked into his office and sat down in one of his guest chairs.

"Hi, Georgia. What can I do for you?" he asked.

"Oh, I just wanted to ask you a few questions about the changes we're making on the website. Plus, I need to get a copy of your bio again. I seem to have lost it in my email Inbox," she said with a lighthearted laugh.

Jim smiled and thought, *I bet Georgia could use a little help from Holly, too.*

"I can certainly send you my latest bio, and then let's set up a time to talk about the website questions. I've got a productivity consultant arriving in just a few minutes so I can't give you any time this morning, but how about after 3 today? Would 3:30 work for you?"

"Sure, 3:30 sounds good. So... you have a productivity consultant, huh? Is that why your office looks so amazing?"

"Oh, you noticed?" Jim said with a smile. "Yes, I couldn't have done it without her. Her name is Holly Goodwin, and we've been working together for a little over a month now. The biggest changes are actually in my computer, but yes, we've certainly made a big difference in my office, too," Jim said proudly.

"It looks great!" Georgia said as she looked around his office. "I was wondering what you were up to. I guess I didn't see Holly coming and going and didn't know how all this came about. Could she do the same thing for me?" She laughed.

"Sure! She'll be here any minute. I'll introduce you. Oh, and I should also show you how she did my filing system." Jim turned his chair toward his credenza and pulled open a drawer. "Check this out. I didn't know file drawers could look this good." Georgia got up from her chair and walked around his desk.

"Oh my! Everything is so organized!" Georgia said. "I couldn't tell you what's in my files these days."

"Yeah, I would have said the same thing last month, but now I can find what I need in seconds and everything I *don't* need is gone. I love it! Same for the documents in my computer—they're completely organized too," Jim said, looking up at Georgia.

"Wow. Sounds great!" Georgia said as she went back to the guest chair and sat down.

"And while my office looks great and all my files are in order, what really made the difference for me was building my new Task List," said Jim as Georgia continued to listen with interest. "It guides me through my day and really keeps me focused on the things I need to do from day to day.

"And today, Holly and I are going to tackle my email Inbox. I've got more than 5,000 emails in there and Holly tells me I'll get that to zero by the time she's finished with me." Just then Jim noticed that Holly had arrived at his office door, escorted by Susan from the front desk. "And speaking of Holly, here she is. Isn't that right, Holly? Zero in the Inbox?"

"That's right, Jim!" Holly said with a big smile.

Georgia stood and introduced herself to Holly, then sat back down in the guest chair. "Holly, I'm curious about what Jim said. Zero in the Inbox? Is that possible? And is it really that important?"

Holly sat in the second guest chair. "Yes, it's possible, and yes, it's important to your overall productivity and progress," she said.

"I just keep everything in my Inbox and then I know I can find what I need with a *Search*." Georgia shrugged. "It seems to work just fine."

"Up until recently, I did that too," Jim said quickly. "But it always took me a lot of time and a *Search* didn't necessarily give me what I was looking for. Have you ever had to run a *Search* on your *Search* results?" Jim asked with a laugh. When Georgia raised her eyebrows and tilted her head, Jim knew she probably had. "But after today, it's going to be a whole new ball game."

Georgia turned to Holly. "I guess I'm still not convinced. Why would I need to get my Inbox down to zero?"

"There are many reasons," Holly began. "First, an Inbox is an _Inbox_. It's a communication tool that's meant to bring information IN. It's not a file cabinet and it's not a to-do list. Everything that comes into an Inbox should go back out again, because an Inbox is not the final destination. Picture the physical Inbox most professionals have on their desks. Imagine trying to find something in that Inbox if you let every piece of mail pile up. That would be kind of difficult to use, right? And the pile could be sky high! Everything coming into an Inbox of any kind—whether for email, voice mail or snail mail—must be processed out to another location."

Georgia nodded. "Good point. I hadn't thought about my email Inbox that way."

"Secondly, with too much stored in your Inbox, you can lose a lot of time looking for things, as Jim has already mentioned. You're not alone in running searches to find emails and attachments, but it's best to get all of the information you receive into better, more effective locations for reference or action. Georgia, have you ever lost track of to-dos coming from emails because something important scrolled off the screen and after that it was out of sight, out of mind?"

"Oh, definitely," Georgia responded. "Not very often, but it's happened. And I don't remember any specific details, but it wasn't disastrous."

"What do you use to keep track of things to do?" asked Holly.

"I use legal pads mostly. Why?"

"That's quite common," Holly nodded. "Many of my clients, including Jim, used legal pads before we started our work together. But here's the issue: When you use paper, legal pads, and post-it notes to keep track of things to do, and keep paper and files on your desk as the reminders themselves, and you have other to-dos coming from email—how do you plan and prioritize action on all of that?" She looked at Georgia.

Georgia shook her head. "I'm not sure."

"The answer is… you can't. Not effectively, anyway. Most professionals *don't* operate with a digital Task List like the one Jim has now, and that means they're really gambling with their productivity. They've got tasks, to-dos and reminders in a dozen places and there's no plan of action. A really effective Task List, like the one Jim is using now, is essential to document everything you need to do all in one place. Not all in one day, but all in one system.

"And when it comes to the Inbox, many professionals are keeping everything—a mix of reference information, action steps and things that should be deleted." Holly turned to Jim. "And you recently found out how much could be deleted from your email folders. Isn't that right, Jim?"

Jim nodded, looking at Georgia. "Honestly, it was surprising. I had NO idea how much I was holding onto that I *didn't* need."

Holly turned to Georgia. "Getting your Inbox to zero begins with setting up reliable systems, like a Task List, Contacts, a Calendar and an e-document library. Then you can more easily make decisions about what you receive in your Inbox and move emails and information into those systems while deleting what you don't need. That's how you can get your Inbox to zero, but you can't do that without all of the other systems in place first, especially the Task List."

Jim looked over at Georgia. She nodded and seemed to be listening intently. He too was gaining a new appreciation for how Taskology worked.

Taskology Tip #14

Your email Inbox is an INbox. It's not a file cabinet and it's not a to-do list. Everything you receive in your Inbox must go somewhere else—to another location for either reference or action—or it's archived or deleted.

"Georgia, getting to zero in the Inbox," Holly continued "means you've *seen* everything, made *decisions* on everything, and you've moved *everything* out of the Inbox and into better systems for either reference or action. It puts you in control because you're 100% aware of everything you've received and where it is. Nothing will slip through the cracks. Nothing will be missed, lost or forgotten. That's the power of an empty Inbox."

"That sounds... great!" Georgia said. "I had no idea that was possible."

"Most people don't," Holly said. "But that's OK. That's why I'm here. I help leaders just like Jim increase their productivity and progress by mastering workload management." Holly turned to Jim and asked, "How do you feel so far, Jim?"

"I feel great! It's amazing, Georgia," he said, looking at her. "I can't believe how different my workdays are now, compared to what they were like just a month or two ago. I've shared a couple of things with you already, but I can show you more when you visit this afternoon. I'll show you my Task List and my e-document library and my email." Georgia seemed interested in knowing more, so Jim was proud to offer a show-and-tell.

"I'd love to see all that, Jim," Georgia said. "I'll be back at 3:30 for our appointment. And Holly, it was great to meet you. You've given me a lot to think about. I'll let you two get started now."

Georgia left Jim's office, and Jim commented to Holly that he'd been thinking about the entire leadership team at Octagon and how they would really benefit from working with her. He added that the next time John, the President, was in the office, he wanted to introduce her.

"That would be great, Jim. I'd love to meet John. And if he's interested, we can talk more about team training. I have just the training series that could help your leadership team. For now, though, let's get back to you so we can get your Inbox closer to zero today. Are you ready?"

"Absolutely! Let's get started." Jim rubbed his hands together in anticipation. This was the part he'd been looking forward to for weeks, and he was confident that tackling his Inbox would allow him to take his productivity to an entirely new level.

"OK, Jim," Holly began, "as I mentioned earlier to Georgia, everything you receive in your email Inbox really belongs in another location for reference or action—or it gets archived or deleted. Your Inbox is a tool, not a system, so we're going to move everything out today."

"Well, you'll have your hands full with *my* email Inbox, that's for sure!" Jim said with a laugh.

"*We'll* be fine," Holly said, "because *you'll* be in the driver's seat learning by doing and I'm going to be with you every step of the way."

Holly sat next to Jim at his computer and asked him to go to the bottom of his Inbox to the oldest emails. She saw that Jim had saved emails from more than three years ago through to the current year. She asked Jim how many of the older years of emails would still be useful to him or if any of the information was required to be kept by legal, financial or other records retention guidelines.

"You have a choice here, Jim," Holly began. "If your company encourages *Archiving,* you can archive the older years. Or, if you have the space, you can set up a folder under the Inbox to contain older years and have access to them all of the time and all in one place."

"I could probably *Archive* the older years now," Jim said. "I only need access to this year and one year prior."

Holly agreed to his plan and Jim archived the older years out of the Inbox. Following Holly's instructions, he set up two new folders under the Inbox: one for the current year and one for the prior year, each one using the year as the folder name. Then, she instructed him to move all of the emails from each year into their respective folders, except for the past three and a half months, which would remain in the Inbox.

"Let me clarify…you mean I can move all of my emails up through July into this year's folder?" asked Jim. "But all the ones since August 1st will stay in the Inbox? Is that correct?"

"Yes, and I'll tell you why we do it this way," Holly explained as Jim moved all the emails from January through July out of the Inbox.

"You see, the most recent three to four months of emails are going to hold the most active tasks and useful information. The emails from the prior seven months probably have good information, too, but it's not a good use of our time to go through all of them to check. You can review those months as homework, starting with July and going backwards, until you're comfortable that you've not missed any tasks. What *we'll* do today is review each email from the most recent couple of months so I can teach you what to do with those emails and the information they contain."

"So that's what we're doing today?" Jim asked. Holly got the feeling he was a little overwhelmed by the prospect of reviewing so many emails.

"Yes, but don't worry, you're going to get *really good* and *really fast* at making decisions on your emails. That's part of the lesson. I want you to quickly make decisions instead of just keeping everything, whether you need it or not. You'll find some of the same kinds of information you discovered when we were reviewing your email folders, too, like contact information, event or meeting information, reading, reference and more. But the fun part about today is finding tasks, and then I'm going to show you how to get those emails with tasks on the Task List. Plus, you'll likely delete *a lot*. You'll see." Holly smiled reassuringly at Jim and then asked him to go back to the bottom of his email Inbox so they could review the emails starting with August.

Jim said he didn't regularly use his Reading pane, but Holly recommended it for today's exercise so he could quickly see each email message without opening them one at a time. Once Jim began his review, he immediately started making quick decisions. Because of the practice he'd gained working on his email folders, he knew where to put the information he wanted to keep. He deleted a lot of emails, too, clearly seeing that many were unnecessary.

Holly observed as Jim reviewed each email, asking him questions along the way. He saved some emails in his newly organized email folders and saved useful attachments, such as reports, spreadsheets and product information, in his electronic document library. When the email itself was unnecessary, he simply saved the attachments and deleted the email. Other emails were deleted once valuable contact information was saved in Contacts. When Jim reached one specific email from late August, though, he stopped and stared at his screen.

"This email came in months ago and I totally forgot about it. I still need to do something about this. And you don't want me to flag it, right?" asked Jim.

"That's correct," Holly said. "You don't need to flag it, because flags aren't useful—they're not going to do anything for you. The flag only highlights an email to tell you there's something important to revisit, but it doesn't help you plan when you'll do it, prioritize it with all of your other tasks, or actually get it done. There's a much more effective way to handle these to-dos, and now is the time for me to show you how. First, what's your task on this one?"

"I need to follow-up with this guy who was introduced to me by a customer and he could be a prospect." said Jim. "It's too bad I forgot about this, but I'm glad to see it now."

"Yes!" Holly agreed. "Better late than never." Then Holly proceeded to show Jim the variety of ways to click and drag an email to his Task List to create a new task. She explained the difference between the *left-click-and-drag* process and the *right-click-and-drag* process and why it was important to stick with the *right-click-and-drag* process most often.

"Jim, once you *right-click-and-drag* an email down to the Task icon on the lower left-hand corner of your email screen, a menu will appear and you'll have several options to choose from. Before I get into the differences between the menu options, I want you to know that by clicking and dragging an email to Tasks—essentially taking that email to the Task List—Outlook will automatically open up a new task for you. But first you'll choose from the menu options that allow you different ways to manage that email."

"I can click and drag an email into the Task List? I didn't know you could do that!" Jim said with amazement.

"Many people don't," Holly replied. "Most are only familiar with the email flag—or they mark their email as *unread* so it stands out in bold font—and they aren't aware that there's a more powerful way to manage emails."

"Can you click and drag an email to the Calendar, too?" Jim asked.

"Yes, and you'll know how to do that after I show you how it works with the Task List, because that's also a very useful process to get emails out of your Inbox that are related to upcoming appointments."

"That's what I was thinking. But I'll wait and see how this works with the Task List first. OK, I'm ready..."

Holly could tell that Jim's wheels were spinning in his mind. She was excited for him, knowing he would quickly embrace this process as soon as he understood it.

To begin, Holly asked Jim to *right-click-and-drag* the email he had discovered, which still required action, to the Task icon at the bottom left corner of his screen and then let go. A small menu appeared and Holly explained the differences between the various menu options.

"Jim, this first option, *Copy Here as Task with Text,* will give you

Taskology Tip #15

To-dos that come from emails should be included on your Task List so you can plan and prioritize them with everything else you need to do.

the exact same outcome as a *left-click-and-drag*. It plugs the text of the email into the Notes section of a new Task, and that's all. Sometimes, that's all you need for your task, but it's not optimal most of the time." Holly asked Jim to cancel out of the menu and do a *left-click-and-drag* on the same email so he could see what the new task looked like. "It's not bad," she continued, "but it doesn't give you the *actual* email in your task, which is what you want at your fingertips when you're ready to work on the task."

Copy Here as Task with Text

Copy Here as Task with Attachment

Move Here as Task with Attachment

Cancel

The Right-Click-and-Drag Menu

Holly then asked Jim to -do a *right-click-and-drag* on the same email and select Option 2 in the menu, *Copy Here as Task with Attachment,* so he could see the result. "Using Options 2 and 3 on this menu will allow you to attach an email to a new task, as you can see. Once the email is there, you can open it up to look at it again, reply to it, forward it, and access the attachments within the email. And when you go back to the Inbox after completing the set-up of this task, you'll still see this email there because Option 2 is a *copy* process.

When you select Option 3—*Move Here as Task with Attachment*—it will literally move the email out of your Inbox because it's a *move* process.

"Should I use Option 3 all the time?" Jim asked.

"It depends," Holly responded with a smile. "Here's the difference between the two. In order to decide whether to use Option 2 or Option 3, think about whether you'll need that email *after* the task is completed or not. For example, will you need this specific email after you finish with this task?"

"Actually, yes," Jim replied. "I'd like to keep this one in an email folder, because it's about a potential prospect."

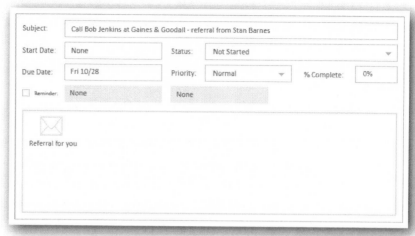

A New Task Created from Options 2 or 3 on the Right-Click-and-Drag Menu

"OK, then in this case you would select Option 2, *Copy Here as Task with Attachment* because once you set up your task with the email attached, you'll return to your Inbox right away and file that email in your *Prospects* folder. That's your process using Option 2. That's the whole point of having it on your Task List—you don't need to see that email in your Inbox anymore as a reminder of something to do."

"Got it," he said. "And if I said I *didn't* need the email after my task was finished, I should use Option 3, which is a *Move*, right?"

"Correct. When you don't need an email later for any reason after a task is completed, you can use Option 3—*Move Here as Task with Attachment*—and simultaneously get the email out of your Inbox. When you finish setting up your task on the Task List and return to your Inbox, that email will already be gone."

"I love it!" Jim said. "This is so cool! Now I can see how I'll get my Inbox to zero."

Holly smiled. She could almost see the proverbial light bulb come on in Jim's head. Just like all of her other clients, Jim was excited about the idea of putting his emails in the best possible locations for reference and action, where they could be most useful, instead of letting them pile up in a tangled mess in the Inbox.

"Just remember that before you *move* an email to the Task List, you want to be sure you *don't* need it later, because once you move it to the Task List, that's the only place it will be. And when you finish your task and delete it, the email will go with it, too."

"Understood," Jim said. "I'm excited about this. I can't wait to get through the rest of my Inbox."

Holly was pleased to see that Jim's initial sense of overwhelm had disappeared and he was excited about the process. "OK, let's continue. Now that you know what your options are, you can finish setting up *this* task using Option 2, since you said you'll need this email later for reference. When we finish setting up the task, the email will still be in your Inbox so you can immediately file it."

"Right," he said.

"OK, we're looking at the new task you just created using Option 2 from the *right-click-and-drag* menu. What do you notice about the Subject field of this task?"

"It's showing the Subject line of the email."

"Exactly. During the process when you click and drag an email to the Task List, the system will automatically plug in the subject line of the email into the Subject field of the new task. Now, is that something you want?" Holly quizzed.

"No?" Jim said. "But I'm not sure."

"No, you don't," Holly said. "After you click and drag an email to the Task List and a new task box opens, your first step is to wipe out the subject line of the email and replace it with *your* action step—what *you're* going to do. Part or all of the subject line from the email may be irrelevant, because it's from an email someone else sent you, and what they've put in the Subject line may have *nothing* to do with your next action step. This is *your* task now, so you must articulate what you're going to do. So, what's your next action step?"

Jim deleted the contents of the Subject field and typed his task, using a verb and adding then details he wanted to remember later on. Then he selected a *Do Date* and clicked *Save & Close*. Once he finished, Holly continued.

"Excellent. Now you know how to get an email to your Task List so it can join the rest of your tasks. When your tasks are all together, you can more effectively plan and prioritize all you need to do."

"So… awesome…" Jim said as he went back to his Inbox and filed the email. "I'm going to have a lot more to add to the Task List!" Jim paused for a moment to consider how many tasks he may add and have to plan for the future. "What if I don't know what *Do Dates* to choose?"

"Each time you're ready to process a number of emails," Holly said, "look at your calendar first to have the next week or so in mind. Keep an eye out for days that aren't especially good for working on tasks—like the days when you're in a lot of meetings or you're off site entirely—and don't plan to do tasks on those days. Once you finish processing a batch of emails, you'll go back to your Task List to review it. Don't miss this final step. Whether you had your schedule in mind or not, you'll still need to consider how all of the new tasks stack up against the existing ones that were already on your list. Then you can reprioritize accordingly."

"Got it," Jim said. "How often will I do that?"

"A couple of times during the day. You might process email less often when you're really busy, but it's important to do it at least twice a day, and preferably more. I recommend dedicating blocks of time for working on tasks and processing email and alternating them throughout your day. Focus on your Task List first—maybe for a half hour to an hour—and knock out one or two important tasks. Then go back to your Inbox and process the new emails that have come in. After you get your email Inbox to a comfortable level again—which I hope will be near or at zero—you'll go back to your Task List and knock out another task or two. After that, return to your Inbox. The faster you make decisions on emails and process them *out* of the Inbox, the sooner you can get back to your Task List and accomplish your priorities."

"That makes perfect sense," Jim said. "And I can use my protected time blocks for tasks and email, right?"

"Yes," Holly replied. "But you'll need more than just your time blocks to work on tasks and email throughout the day. Those time blocks just represent your *uninterrupted time* during the day—when you can shut your door —but you should have more time at your disposal to do all the things you need to do for your job. The biggest challenge my clients have with email is that they don't dedicate enough time during the day to give this process the time it needs. As a result, their email can build up again.

"I don't want my Inbox to build up again after this," Jim said. "And I like the idea of focusing on one thing at a time—the Task List or email. Before, all I did was bounce back and forth from moment to moment between the Inbox and ringing phones and visitors while trying to get things done. Or worse, I'd get stuck in the Inbox and never get out!"

"Sounds familiar," Holly agreed. "Most professionals bounce around too much and can get stuck in the Inbox, too, both of which are inefficient and unproductive. While they're busy reading, answering, deleting or filing emails, they're not necessarily *processing* them the way I've just shown you. They're also not necessarily moving information to all the proper locations for reference and they're not moving emails to a Task List for action. *And...* they're not actually getting emails *out* of the Inbox."

"I know what you mean," Jim said. "That used to be me. But now I know what to do with my email, starting today!"

Jim seemed pleased to have discovered the secret for getting out of email jail. Holly watched as he continued to delete more emails, occasionally moving reference information to other locations and practicing what he had just learned to get emails with to-dos on the Task List. When he *copied* the email to his Task List, he came back to the Inbox right away to file it in one of his email folders. When he *moved* an email to the Task List, it meant he wouldn't need the email after the task was finished, and he could rest assured the email was removed from the Inbox entirely. And sometimes, Jim saved an email or individual attachments in his electronic document library for more long-term reference, and then he deleted it.

Throughout the Inbox review, Jim also found emails containing reading material he hadn't yet read, so he practiced the *Slow Down to Speed Up* lesson Holly had taught him previously. He took a minute to review what he'd received so he could determine the value of the reading and decide what steps to take next. He deleted most of the emails, but two landed on his Task List in separate tasks after he decided they deserved more in-depth reading or may have possible next action steps.

As Jim reached the emails from late October, he suddenly exclaimed, "Aha! I was looking for this the other day and I couldn't find it!"

"What is it?" asked Holly.

"It's an email from a customer shopping for new scanners for their business. When I recently asked her about getting a response to my proposal, she said she'd already responded and was waiting on me. But I never saw her email! And here it is! I don't know how I missed this. I'm sure my eyes crossed the other day when I tried to find it. I am *so* glad I finally solved this mystery."

"Good to hear, Jim," Holly said. "There's nothing like finding something you were looking for. Now you can move forward."

Since Jim already had a task on his Task List for this customer, Holly shared another lesson with him. Using this email he had fortuitously found, she showed him how to insert an email into a task that was *already* on his Task List. Holly explained that rather than doing the click-and-drag procedure, which was used only for creating *new* tasks, this process would start with the existing task and use the *Insert* feature within. When he finished, Jim returned to the Inbox and filed the email in a folder for this customer.

As Jim got closer to November, the more tasks he found and added to his Task List. And the more tasks he added, the more he sighed. Holly became somewhat concerned. "Are you OK, Jim?"

"Yeah... I just don't even want to look at all the stuff I've added to my Task List now. There's going to be so much!" Jim seemed a little overwhelmed, which Holly sometimes witnessed, even with the most excited of clients.

"Jim, don't worry. This Task List will help you feel *more* in control, not *less*. And you'll feel so good about having all of your tasks on your Task List in one place—where you can effectively manage them—*and* having an empty Inbox. Not that your Inbox will stay that way," Holly smiled, "but you *know* how to process emails now and you can move them all *out*, starting today. We'll look at your Task List in a few minutes so you can reprioritize everything and we'll adjust your daily task plan so it's realistic and doable—a plan you'll be comfortable with, OK?"

"OK," Jim said. "I'm all right. I just can't imagine how much I need to catch up on."

"Oh, it's not that much. But even if it were, you have the power to prioritize now. That's the best part about the Task List. You can't do everything today, even if you feel like you *should*. During this catch-up phase you won't have to overload too many days with tasks, and when you can protect the right amount of time to get it under control, this phase will be short-lived. Then, going forward, you'll know exactly how much time you need each day to stay on top of your tasks *and* process your emails. It will all become very clear."

"Sounds good!" Jim said with a smile.

At that point, Holly noticed the time and she could see that they wouldn't get to all of Jim's emails in the Inbox today. "Jim, we're just about out of time, but we'll pick up with this again next week when I come back. What you can do in the meantime is keep practicing what you learned today. Keep taking emails to the Task List and remember to alternate your time blocks spent working on tasks and processing emails, OK?"

Jim agreed and looked forward to continuing so he could finally get his Inbox to zero. When Holly returned the following week, Jim showed her that he had not only kept up with recent emails from the past week, but had also made more progress on the emails from the past as well.

"And look, you're in November, Jim! You're almost there!" Holly said with encouragement.

"Yeah, not much left now!" Jim said.

Holly instructed Jim to continue with the process and as she watched, she guided him through various other lessons, including how to add multiple emails to the same task, whether new or existing, and how to save multiple attachments at the same time in his electronic document library. And when Jim found relevant information he wanted to add to his Calendar, Holly showed him how to use the *right-click-and-drag* process to create new appointments as well as how to attach emails to existing appointments on his Calendar.

Finally Jim reached the end of the process and achieved an empty Inbox. "I did it. I can't believe it," he said. "I haven't seen an empty Inbox since I started here, and *that* didn't last very long. Thank you so much for showing me how to do this. And you were right... I feel so good!"

After congratulating Jim and letting him relish his achievement, Holly instructed him to revisit the *Action* folder in his email folders list, which contained emails with to-dos or follow-ups. A couple weeks ago, Holly had asked

Jim to skip this folder, because she knew they would address it today. Jim looked through all the emails in the *Action* folder and was relieved to see that he had already completed most of the to-dos. For the few remaining emails that needed action, he added them to the Task List and prioritized them with the rest of his tasks. Once the *Action* folder was empty, Jim deleted it, knowing his Task List was now the go-to method for planning, prioritizing and accomplishing tasks.

Holly then asked Jim to revisit his Task List for the final step that shouldn't be missed: *reprioritizing*. She told him that no matter how many tasks he added in one sitting, he should immediately revisit the Task List to see how many tasks were now showing for each day. Given that he could only do so many tasks on any given day, he could compare new and existing tasks, determine which tasks should be accomplished sooner than later, and change *Do dates* accordingly. This final step would keep his Task List up-to-date, realistic and achievable.

Jim took a minute to reprioritize tasks according to their priority and urgency. Once he finished he said, "You were right. I feel so much better now. I'm aware of *everything* and I can prioritize all of it so easily. I really do have a handle on *everything* I need to do!"

"That's right, Jim!" Holly said. "And remember, you'll do this process a few times a day. As you get more emails, phone calls, and things to do, you'll continue to add them to your Task List and reprioritize, plus remove other tasks as they're completed. As the day goes by, the list should reflect any changes that have occurred for your priorities. When you keep using the list, it will never let you down. It will always give you total clarity about what you need to do and when. You'll be in control of your time and you'll have confidence that you're zeroing in on your real priorities, while nothing is missed, lost or forgotten. How will that feel?" Holly hoped to reconfirm the connection between Jim's daily use of the Task List and this new email process with all the resulting benefits.

"It'll feel great!" Jim said. "It feels great already. I feel a lot less stressed knowing I've seen everything in my Inbox and that I have an action plan. There's no chance of forgetting or missing anything, and that feels so good. I have so much more peace of mind."

Jim clicked on his email icon to enjoy seeing his empty Inbox again, but instead he saw two new emails that had just arrived.

"Oh, look!" Holly laughed. "More emails are already coming in. But this time you have a step-by-step process to use and you know what to do with everything that lands in your Inbox, right?"

"That's right," Jim said with complete confidence. "They don't have to sit here and build up anymore."

Jim's smile said it all. Holly never tired of seeing her clients get to this stage of the consulting, when relief had arrived, satisfaction was apparent, and peace of mind had settled in. At this stage, clients finally felt less burdened and less stressed, and could celebrate the end of chaos, confusion and clutter in all its forms...for good.

Chapter 15 Summary

- **An email Inbox is an _Inbox_. It's not a file cabinet and it's not a to-do list.** It's a communication tool that's meant to bring emails in. Everything that comes into an Inbox must go back out again to another location for reference or action.

- **A lot of time is lost in a professional workday when searching for emails.** When too many emails accumulate in an Inbox, they start scrolling off the screen and important things can be missed: opportunities, follow-ups, tasks, reminders, events, information, and more.

- **Keeping a low or empty email Inbox** means you've read or reviewed every email, made a decision about the value of the information within the email, and you've moved the information you're keeping into a better location for reference or action. Nothing is missed, lost, or forgotten, and nothing slips through the cracks.

- **Include to-dos from emails on your Task List** so you can plan and prioritize them with everything else you need to do.

- **How to Get to Zero in the Inbox for the first time:**
  - Turn on the Right Side Reading Pane for easy review of emails
  - Move older years out of your Inbox and into Archive folders or move them into new subfolders of the Inbox, named by year or a group of years.
  - Create a folder for the current year and move all but the most recent 3-4 months of emails into it.
  - Review the most recent 3-4 months of emails in your Inbox to look for useful information and tasks.
  - Move valuable information into other systems for reference or action:
    - Move contact information to Contacts
    - Move event or meeting information to the Calendar
    - Save attachments in your electronic document library
    - Move emails to email folders if they should remain in your email system

- ■ Print and file what needs to be stored physically
- ■ Add tasks to your Task List
- o Leave Reading in your Inbox and read or delete everything by the end of the week.
- **Use the Right-Click-and-Drag procedure to copy or move an email with a to-do to the Task List** when it holds an action step for you. If you use the *copy* process, be sure to return to the Inbox file the email immediately.
- **To keep your email Inbox low or at zero at all times**, protect time in your day to process email, and alternate these time blocks with those for working on tasks. After creating a number of tasks from emails, be sure to revisit the Task List to reprioritize and make sure your daily task plan is realistic.

CHAPTER 16

Productivity and Progress

IT WAS 8:45 am on a Wednesday morning two weeks after the appointment when Jim had cleared out his Inbox. Holly had given Jim two weeks between appointments to continue using and practicing the new systems and processes of Taskology. During this time, Jim felt he'd done a great job and was truly benefiting from his new level of workload management and making more progress than ever before.

As Jim sat in his office, waiting for Holly to arrive at 9:00 am, he reflected on the past two months. He knew Holly would ask about his daily use of the system and how he felt about his progress. Jim could easily tell her his workday now seemed light years ahead of where he started.

He'd been using his Task List every day and had gotten into a routine of adding new tasks, updating existing tasks, changing *Do Dates*, and deleting tasks that were entirely completed. He continued to reprioritize as new tasks and priorities came up, and he added information to the other systems he had access to, such as Contacts, Calendar, email folders, and his electronic document library. Above all, he really enjoyed creating tasks from emails so he could get important to-dos *out* of his Inbox and onto the Task List where he could prioritize them with everything else on his list.

Jim felt like he was saving so much time because he wasn't searching for emails or attachments anymore, he wasn't shuffling papers or files on his desk, and he wasn't missing to-dos or follow-ups. He now had a place for everything and a process to follow for all of his reference information and action steps. As he continued to use the system, he continued to feel more and more in control of his workday.

Unforeseen issues or emergencies had popped up every so often, of course, but Jim had been prepared. He was able to turn on a dime and regroup in an instant. He could respond quickly to the requests of others without random reactivity and without forgetting something important. And for once, the last-minute issues weren't *caused* by his disorganization or lack of a plan.

Jim had learned from Holly that the point of the Taskology Task List wasn't just about having a plan for what to do each day. It was also about having the ability to choose what *not* to do. He realized that this new system for tracking *all* of his tasks and priorities gave him the power and freedom to choose which tasks to accomplish now and which tasks to accomplish later, without losing track of anything. From moment to moment he had the ability to decide to do a new, higher-priority tasks that had surfaced suddenly instead of other tasks he'd originally planned to do.

Jim now understood that having a complete Task List would support him in making informed decisions about how to spend his time, which was one of the most important resources he could use to increase his productivity and progress. He felt good knowing he didn't have to struggle to remember what to do each day and could avoid the panic that used to take over when he'd forgot something important.

As Jim surfaced from his reflection, he realized Holly would arrive any minute, so he quickly grabbed a cup of coffee and went to the lobby in anticipation of her timely arrival. Sure enough, a minute before 9:00 am, Holly walked in and greeted Jim with a smile.

"I'm ready for my check-up!" he laughed as they turned and walked down the hall to his office.

"How's everything going?" she asked as they sat down.

"Wonderfully!" Jim said. "I love the system. I really do. I'm keeping my desk clear, my files and e-files are still working really well, and I get my Inbox to zero every day." Jim turned to his computer to show Holly his empty Inbox, even though two new emails had just arrived. They shared a knowing smile about the never-ending influx of email and Holly congratulated him on a job well done.

"And my Task list keeps me on track every day. I prioritize from day to day and I'm not overloading any days with too many tasks. I'm moving tasks around as my day changes and I try to make it as realistic as possible. Although, sometimes I feel like I'm procrastinating a bit, but I'm not sure."

"Well," Holly began, "remember when we talked about this initially? Let's think about the two possible scenarios—procrastinating and reprioritizing—and confirm the difference between the two. You're reprioritizing if you're really choosing what's *most* important for the day and rearranging your tasks to reflect that. So don't feel like you're cheating or skipping out on work when you're reprioritizing well. If you believe you're spending your precious time on the most important task that will benefit the bottom line, you're making smart decisions.

"However, if you're *not* choosing to spend your time on the tasks that will impact the bottom line in the best possible ways, then that's something to notice. In addition, if you're moving tasks forward—again and again—to a date farther out into the future, then you could be procrastinating. You just need to review the task and see how you phrased it. Check to see if the task reflects too large of a step—or perhaps it shows multiple steps—and should be changed to reflect a *smaller* first or next action step. Or maybe you're trying to do a task too soon. Perhaps it something that really *should* wait several weeks or months before you do it."

Jim nodded as he looked at his list. He felt sure now that he'd been reprioritizing well rather than procrastinating. He was glad Holly could remind him of the differences between the two and felt empowered to catch himself in the future if he were ever to procrastinate.

Jim and Holly continued to talk about the various scenarios Jim had encountered in the past two weeks and she addressed his questions and observations. While they were talking, Kelly Sheraton, the Director of Human Resources, walked into Jim's office.

"Oh, excuse me, Jim," Kelly said immediately, stopping just inside his doorway. "Your door was open, but I didn't realize you had a guest... I just wanted to drop off this file for you to look at. It's for the new performance review process. But I can just leave it for now. I apologize for interrupting your meeting."

"No worries, Kelly," Jim said quickly. "Come on in. There's someone I'd like you to meet."

He formally introduced Holly and Kelly, and they exchanged greetings. Jim invited Kelly to stay for a minute.

"Kelly, Holly and I have been working together on workload management and productivity. You can see my office has changed over the past month or two---"

"Yes, I certainly can!" laughed Kelly. "A few weeks ago I noticed how your office had been transformed. Very impressive!"

"Well, lots of things have been transformed, but my office is the probably the easiest to see," Jim said, smiling. "With Holly's help I've really mastered my work-day. I have a new Task List I'm using to manage all of my to-dos. I have new systems for managing my files and e-files. I have clear open spaces where I can work and think. But the best part— other than the Task List—is having an empty email Inbox, which I haven't had for *years*. Holly showed me how to clear out more than 5,000 emails and taught me a new process for managing emails going forward."

Kelly's eyebrows shot up. "Really? You had 5,000 emails in your Inbox? My gosh! I can hardly deal with having more than 30. I have to have less than a screen-full, so I try not to have more than 15 or 20. Right now I've got about 10 or 15."

"That's wonderful, Kelly!" Holly said. "How many email folders do you have set up?"

"A lot," Kelly said. "Why do you ask?"

"Because when you say *a lot* it tells me you could be holding onto too many emails and you may be over-organizing, which can cost you more time when you go to file things or look for things later. But, that aside, what's more important are the emails sitting in your Inbox. What do the usual 15 or 20 emails represent? Why are they sitting there?"

"Oh, they're just there because I need to do something with them," Kelly said matter-of-factly.

"Right," Holly said. "I bet you try to take care of them as *soon* they appear, right? And sometimes they back up just a little bit?"

"Yeah, it's just easier to knock them out as soon as they show up. And if I can't get to them right away, I leave them in the Inbox until I can work on them, which is usually fairly soon."

Holly nodded, and Jim guessed she'd probably heard this scenario many times before.

"Did you know you're giving up something important when you take action *right away* on each and every email as it comes in?" Holly asked.

"No…what is it?" Kelly asked, shaking her head slightly.

"The power to prioritize," Holly said. "When you address every email as soon as it arrives in your Inbox, you're spending time on it whether it's a true priority or not, whether it's the best use of your time or not, and whether it furthers your own agenda or not.

"You see, it's important to take into account the level of priority of the tasks that are coming from those emails. You may be jumping in to take care of them as soon as they appear—or as soon as you can do something—because you have nowhere else to put them. When the emails stay in your Inbox, you're also not comparing those tasks with all the other existing tasks you had to do. Now, if we were to classify your approach, would you say it was more *proactive* or *reactive*?"

"Probably… reactive," Kelly said with a smile.

"That's right," Holly confirmed. "You're being more *reactive* than *proactive* from day to day and *living from your Inbox*. It's like working in short-order deli, where every sub or sandwich is made as soon as it's ordered by a customer who's just walked up to the deli counter. There's no priority to making the sandwiches, because it's *first come, first served*, which is the same as taking care of every task as soon as you see it."

"You know, I hadn't thought about that before? So, *first come, first served* is fine for making sandwiches, but for tasks---" said Kelly, as she paused and looked at Holly.

"---there must be a sense of priority," Holly continued. "And if you're not comparing what you receive in your email Inbox with everything else you need to do, then you're not *proactively* making decisions about what your real priorities are or how to spend your valuable time, are you?"

"No… I guess not," Kelly said slowly, a puzzled look on her face. "A short-order deli is a good way to describe how I deal with my email. And I guess that's not the best way to manage them… " Kelly looked at Jim.

"I know," Jim said to Kelly. "I've been there myself, but now everything is completely different. I have almost nothing in my Inbox, I got rid of dozens of email folders, and I can work from a Task List that really works. I'll always have emails coming in, of course, but now I know what to do with them and I know when to give my Inbox and my Task List the time and attention they need."

Kelly nodded. "This is all new to me, but I like the sounds of everything you and Holly have said. I might ask Holly to work with me!"

"Smart move!" Jim said. "I'm going to introduce Holly to John and see if we can offer a *Taskology for Teams* Training for my sales team."

"Sounds good," Kelly said. "I think everyone could benefit from a lot less email, a lot more time, and a better way to get things done."

Jim looked over at Holly, and she just smiled. He knew Holly would be able to help plenty of people improve their workload management skills and boost productivity and progress at Octagon Office Solutions.

—— ❦ ——

CHAPTER 17

Enjoying a New Kind of Vacation

The sun felt warm on Jim's face as he leaned back in a comfortable beach chair alongside his wife, Julie.

"This week has been wonderful, Jim," said Julie, reaching over to take his hand. "I just realized we're halfway through our vacation and you haven't had to talk to anyone at work even once."

"I know. Hasn't it been great?" Jim said. "This is the first time in years I've been able to disconnect from work and decompress on a vacation. I promised this vacation would be different, remember? Over the past few months I've changed so many things and now my work is totally under control."

"Yeah, you did say all that. But honestly, honey, after the vacations we've had in recent years, I didn't dare believe it. Can I ask a small favor?"

"Of course. Name it."

"Whatever you're doing differently at work, please keep doing it."

Jim chuckled and squeezed Julie's hand. "Don't worry. I intend to."

He took the last sip of his iced tea and laid back in his beach chair. Yeah, Florida really was the perfect choice for this Spring Break getaway. He smiled, remembering how excited their daughters had been at the news. What a terrific way to escape the late March snow and cold weather still lingering at home.

But Jim didn't need to think about home. He didn't need to think about work, either. While he'd been enjoying his vacation, he hadn't had to think about his tasks or his emails or anything else related to Octagon Office Solutions. For the first time in years, he wasn't receiving any panicked phone calls from his team or from Jennifer, his assistant, and he hadn't burned up valuable vacation time dealing with unforeseen issues or emergencies. At that moment, the only thing on his mind was how warm the sand was under his feet, and his most pressing task was getting another bottle of iced tea from the cooler.

In past years, the days prior to vacations were always spent frantically trying to address last-minute questions and issues, and then during his week of vacation he typically heard from the office at least five times, if not more. But so far, he hadn't heard from anyone—and he didn't expect to. He attributed this to his work with Holly and his proactive steps prior to leaving for vacation.

In the week before he left, Jim closed as many open loops as possible, and alerted everyone in the office that he'd be on vacation for a week. He sent half a dozen emails to various people—including his sales team and Jennifer—to delegate tasks, share important information, give updates, and remind them of his upcoming absence. He requested that no one contact him while he was away, but made sure everyone he was currently working with knew how to contact Jennifer in case they needed anything.

Jim emptied his Inbox before Friday had ended and made sure all of his tasks on the Task List were prioritized for the days and weeks following his return. He was aware he'd have a lot of email to process after his vacation, but this time, the idea of post-vacation email cleanup didn't worry him. He had purposely protected his first day back at the office and kept it free from meetings so he could catch up with his team and with Jennifer, and get his Inbox back to zero using the process Holly had taught him.

It had helped, too, that after completing the consulting sessions with Holly, Jim had enrolled in Holly's coaching program so he could keep his productivity and progress on track. After creating an entirely new kind of workday for himself, he wanted to protect the system that now supported him and receive continued coaching for new situations.

Throughout the winter months, Jim had been able to sail along with Taskology, and when Julie asked about surprising their daughters with a spring break vacation in Florida, Jim felt comfortable taking the week off to be with his family. And so did John, his boss.

When Jim left his office on the Friday afternoon before vacation, Jim felt confident that no tasks, jobs or projects were left hanging, and there was no chance he'd missed or forgotten anything. He didn't expect to receive any calls from the office or have to call in after suddenly remembering something while he was sitting on the beach. No, not on this vacation.

As he soaked up the sun and listened to his kids play in the sand nearby, Jim was thrilled he'd been able to keep his promise to Julie. He hadn't spent any time talking on the phone or compulsively checking his email. That had been a sore spot between them on every vacation, and this time he was determined it would be different. He deserved a work-free week of vacation, and his wife and kids deserved more quality time with him.

As Jim settled into his morning routine on the Monday following his vacation, he was pleasantly surprised to find there were no issues to resolve and no fires to put out. His team, colleagues and assistant had been able to carry on with his instructions, take care of business and look after customers.

Jim remembered how apprehensive he'd always been about returning to work after taking time off, knowing he'd have to suffer through a tumultuous *re-entry* period. But this time, thanks to Taskology, he'd been more proactive in closing open loops, prioritizing tasks, and creating a plan for his absence and return. As a result, he was more productive both before *and* after his vacation—something he hadn't experienced before.

Jim was quite pleased with this new kind of vacation and the post-vacation period. How nice it was to finally be able to smoothly and seamlessly return to his workday—almost as if he'd never been away.

Jim sipped his coffee and smiled.

Summary of Taskology Tips

Taskology Tip #1
The two most important questions to ask when planning tasks:
1. *What* am I going to do?
2. *When* am I going to do it?

Taskology Tip #2
Build a single, digital Task List to consolidate and document everything you need to do so you can effectively plan and prioritize all tasks. (Not all in one day. All in one *system*.)

Taskology Tip #3
Your day will never be static and therefore your Task List will never be static. Your Task List will change to reflect new tasks and priorities, changes to existing tasks, and the deletion of completed tasks.

Taskology Tip #4
The Task-Time Connection
The number of tasks you plan to do each day should fit within the amount of time you have available. If you need more time, *protect* more time, but avoid planning to do more tasks than your time will allow.

Taskology Tip #5
Clutter represents a build-up of unmade or deferred decisions. Keep making decisions about everything you receive, whether physically or electronically.

Taskology Tip #6
Reach for the S.T.A.R.R.s
S – Send it out
T – Toss it
A – Act on it
R – Reference it
R – Read it

Taskology Tip #7
Reading
Read what you set aside to read within the week you receive it, because more reading is already on its way to you. At the end of the week, if you still haven't read it, toss or delete it. You're not getting any value from it just by keeping it.

Taskology Tip #8
Pending Tasks
"Pending" tasks or things you're "waiting for" almost always turn back into action for you. Add follow-ups to your Task List with a target date of action so nothing will be missed, lost or forgotten.

Taskology Tip #9
Taskology Priorities
   1 = Revenue-generating
   2 = Important
   3 = It would be nice if...

Taskology Tip #10
It's important to have a calendar that is both clear and accurate – without confusion, duplicates or clutter – so you know exactly where you'll be and for how long.

Taskology Tip #11
Protect Your Time
Maintaining an all-day, open-door policy all day is inefficient and costly. Block a minimum of two hours of uninterrupted time per day on your calendar so you're reminded that you need that time. You don't want others to steal it and you don't want to give it away too quickly.

Taskology Tip #12
The less you keep, the less you have to manage and the more time you'll save for yourself.

Taskology Tip #13

Your email folders list should be short and visible on one screen. The structure begins with two main folders —"Business" and "Personal"—as sub-folders of the Inbox. Major Category folders within "Business" and "Personal" are named for broad categories such as projects, programs, jobs, clients, vendors or departments. Sub-folders may or may not be necessary to further sub-categorize emails within Major Category folders.

Taskology Tip #14

Your email Inbox is an INbox. It's not a file cabinet and it's not a to-do list. Everything you receive in your Inbox must go somewhere else—to another location for either reference or action—or it's archived or deleted.

Taskology Tip #15

To-dos that come from emails should be included on your Task List so you can plan and prioritize them with everything else you need to do.

Chapter Summaries

Chapter 5 Summary

- **Use your Task List for** *task management,* not *project management,* and focus on taking small action steps to move tasks forward.
- **The two most important questions to ask when planning tasks are:**
  - ○ *What am I going to do?*
  - ○ *When am I going to do it?*

  Your answers will address the "what" and "when" of getting things done.
- **Focus on when you'll *do* a task, not when it's *due.***
- Enter your task in the *Subject* field and use the *Due Date* field for your *Do Date,* which is the date you plan to take action. This is the first level of priority for a task.
- Always determine if there is a ***next action step*** you need to take before deleting a task. If there *is* a next action step, either revise the original task or add a new task. Then add a *Do Date* to show your target date of action.
- **Delete tasks when they are *truly* complete,** with no further action steps. Don't accumulate *Completed Tasks* unnecessarily.

Chapter 6 Summary

- **Build a single, digital Task List to consolidate and contain everything** you need to do so you can effectively compare and prioritize all tasks in one system. (Not all in one day. All in one *system*.)

- Your day will never be static and therefore **your Task List will never be static**. Your Task List will change to reflect new tasks and priorities, changes to existing tasks, and the deletion of completed tasks.

- **Detailed descriptions will support you best** when planning and prioritizing tasks. Always include *who*, *what* and *why* in the task description.

- *S.A.V.E.D. by Your Task List* is a tool to remember the necessary elements to include when planning tasks and adding them to your Task List.

  - ○ **S** – *Summarize* your task
  - ○ **A** – Identify your *Action step*
  - ○ **V** – Start every task with a *Verb*
  - ○ **E** – *Enter* a...
  - ○ **D** – *Date*

- **Planning to do five or six tasks per day** is a good place to start before you learn how to manage interruptions and distractions, and learn how to protect more time in your day for getting things done.

- **The Task-Time Connection:** The number of tasks you plan to do each day should match the time you have available. If you need more time, *protect* more time, but don't plan to do more tasks than your time will allow.

Chapter 7 Summary

- **Paper** is a tool, not a system. Save time and work more efficiently and effectively by using a digital Task List instead of writing and re-writing to-do lists on paper.
- **Clutter** is collection of unmade or deferred decisions. Keep making decisions about everything you receive, whether physically or digitally, and move things forward.
- **Slow Down to Speed Up**
  Slow down to read or review the items you receive so you can make decisions about what's useful to you and what's not. Move items you need to keep into better locations for reference or action, and dispense with items you don't need by tossing, archiving or deleting. Generally, it only takes 30-60 seconds to make quick decisions about what's useful to you and where to put it. When you slow down to review and make decisions, you can speed up your productivity and progress in the long run.
- **Dependent Tasks**
  A dependent task is one that requires one or more steps to be taken first and if entered into your Task List, it will hold up your progress. Identify and enter the real *first* or *next* action step on every task and when it's time to take action, you'll move forward without hesitation.

Chapter 8 Summary

- **Reach for the S.T.A.R.R.s:** an acronym to outline where to put items you receive each day in your office.
  - **S = Send it out**
  Just like an Outbox, this is a location on your desk where items can rest until they leave your office, which should occur several times a day. Outgoing items include things to mail out, give away, delegate, or file elsewhere. An actual Outbox is not necessary, but be sure to use a location on the far corner of your desk closest to the door.
  - **T = Toss it**
  Trash cans and recycle bins should be next to or under your desk. Shred bins should be nearby.
  - **A = Act on it**
  An *Action pile* or *Action file* is a location for the papers and files that represent tasks on your Task List while you're not working on them just yet. Keep items in a pile or in a vertical sorter on your desk or credenza, but not in your immediate work space.
  - **R = Reference it**
  Reference locations hold materials you want to reference in the future. Examples include file drawers in your desk and your credenza, or in the file cabinets in your office.
  - **R = Read it**
  The *Reading* pile holds physical reading materials, like magazines and newspapers, and should be kept on your desk or credenza, but not in your immediate work space. Reading should be read as soon as possible in order to gain value from it. Otherwise, it should be discarded. Protect time each week to read, and make sure it disappears by the end of every week, because more reading already on its way.

Chapter 9 Summary

- **Pending tasks** or things you're "waiting for" almost always turn back into action for you. If you set these items aside in a pending pile or "waiting for" file and expect others to follow up, you could lose progress. Add tasks to your Task List to remind you to follow up on anything you're waiting for so tasks won't stall or slip through the cracks.
- **Keep track of how and when you follow up.** Add "lvm" for "left voice mail" at the end of the task and add the date you left the voicemail. Use "sem" for "sent email." These notations will remind you of how and when you last reached out to someone and will be helpful when:
    o You would have otherwise forgotten when and how you last reached out.
    o You're planning how much time to give someone to get back to you before taking action again.
    o Your days get busy with new priorities, issues or emergencies and having the facts at hand helps you prioritize and act more quickly.

Chapter 10 Summary

- **Prioritize tasks within each day by using a 1, 2 or 3 to designate meaning or value.** Most tasks should reflect 2s. The 1s should stand out and the 3s should stand out. When too many tasks have 1s, it means everything is a priority, and then nothing is a priority.
    - **1 = a revenue-generating**, money-making, money-saving, or business-building task. It could be a task that's also be terribly urgent. Overall, a task that gets a 1 is the BEST use of your time.
    - **2 = an important task.** These tasks are requirements of your job. They must be accomplished and keep your daily business moving forward.
    - **3 = "it would be nice if."** These tasks would be *nice to do.* These are tasks that aren't time sensitive or high importance. This kind of task may include certain kinds of reading, video watching, and ideas to consider.
- **ALL tasks (not just some tasks) receive a 1, 2 or 3** so you can instantly recognize the value, meaning or importance of a task, which will help you prioritize with more efficiency and accuracy. Using these will help you ensure you get the right things done at the right time.
- **A 2 can become a 1 and a 3 can become a 2 because of the passage of time or a looming deadline ahead.** When a 2 becomes a 1, it doesn't mean it suddenly became a money-maker, but rather it just became more urgent due to a time constraint. The same applies when a 3 becomes a 2.
- **Your Task List is *Mission Control*.** It holds everything you need to do in one system. Review your list periodically throughout the day to see what you've done and not done, and reprioritize as necessary. Take time to add, change and delete tasks from the list, and adjust tasks that need a new next action step and a new *Do Date*. When you see you're running out of time to accomplish everything on your list for the day, the 3s are the first to be moved.

164

- **By the end of each day, make sure *all* tasks for the day are reprioritized or deleted.**
  If a task is NOT completed by the end of the day, reprioritize it for a more realistic day in the future. If you identify a next action step for a task, rephrase the original task to reflect the new action step and give it a new *Do Date*. If you finish a task, and there are no further action steps, simply delete the task.

Chapter 12 Summary

- **Maintain a calendar that's both clear and accurate**, without confusion, duplicates or clutter, so you know exactly where you'll be each day and for how long.

- **Use the *Week* or *Month* view for viewing your calendar.** The Day view puts blinders on you, limiting your ability to see what's coming up and compromising your ability to plan.

- **Maintaining an all-day, open-door policy is inefficient and costly.** When you allow interruptions without limitation, you're more likely to react to the requests of others instead of being proactive with your own agenda. An open-door policy risks the loss of time, focus, concentration, quality, speed and productivity.

- **Use your *Time Guard* and close your door** for periods of time so you can focus without interruption to get things done. An all-day, open-door policy is fine for 80% of the day, but guard the remaining 20% of your day with a strong commitment to your priorities. Guard this time so others won't steal it and you won't give it away so readily.

- **Protect at least two hours a day**, every day, for uninterrupted time. Schedule these hours separately or together, for doing tasks on your Task List, processing email, or working on special projects.

- **A calendar is for scheduled appointments and commitments.** The Task List is for tasks. Avoid putting tasks on a calendar unless the task will take at least 45-60 minutes or more to do.

- **Look at your calendar first** before adding or reprioritizing tasks so you're aware of the days that are best for accomplishing tasks as well as how many tasks to plan for certain days.

- **"Channeling" is a way to *pull* interruptions into a specific time frame** that works for you rather than to allowing people to *push* them at you all day long. Channel information and questions from others into brief, one-to-one meetings so you can all enjoy fewer interruptions and more focus during the day.

Chapter 14 Summary

- **ORGANIZE, CENTRALIZE and MINIMIZE**
  These are 3 main goals to achieve when taking control of email folders in order to manage reference emails more efficiently and effectively. When these goals are accomplished, you can save a lot of time and energy.
  - **ORGANIZE** email folders that share a similar topic into fewer, but broader Major Category folders. This will consolidate folders and shorten your list. With fewer folders, navigation will be faster and easier, which will save time.
  - **CENTRALIZE** information that belongs elsewhere in other systems for reference or action. Examples include saving contact information into Contacts, adding event or meeting information to the Calendar, saving attachments in your e-document library, and adding tasks to the Task List.
  - **MINIMIZE** the number of emails and email folders you keep. Keep only what's useful to you or what's required by your records retention guidelines, and archive or delete the rest.
- **An email folders list should be short and visible on one screen.** The structure begins with two main folders—*Business* and *Personal*—as sub-folders to the Inbox. Within "Business" and "Personal" are Major Category folders, and within those are sub-folders to further categorize your email. Sub-folders may or may not be necessary for some Major Category folders.
- **Name folders according to how emails are useful to you and what they're for** instead of naming them for who or where the emails came from. Examples include projects, programs, locations, departments, vendors, customers, clients, jobs or other large categories. There are exceptions, of course, such as naming folders for those to whom you delegate tasks regularly. Otherwise, folders should NOT be named for the people who send you emails.

- **Using *Rules* has the potential to hurt your productivity.** You can lose track of the volume of emails coming in—because you never see them in your Inbox—and as a result you may never know what kind of time you need to read or review these emails, process information or plan tasks. *Rules* can prevent you from addressing emails in a timely manner, which can cause you to miss deadlines, lose track of data, and forget follow-ups.

Chapter 15 Summary

- **An email Inbox is an _Inbox_. It's not a file cabinet and it's not a to-do list.** It's a communication tool that's meant to bring emails in. Everything that comes into an Inbox must go back out again to another location for reference or action.

- **A lot of time is lost in a professional workday when searching for emails.** When too many emails accumulate in the Inbox, they start scrolling off the screen and important things can be missed: opportunities, follow-ups, tasks, reminders, events, information, and more.

- **Keeping a low or empty email Inbox** means you've read or reviewed every email, made a decision about the value of the information within the email, and you've moved the information you're keeping into a better location for reference or action. Nothing is missed, lost, or forgotten, and nothing slips through the cracks.

- **Include to-dos from emails on your Task List** so you can plan and prioritize them with everything else you need to do.

- **How to Get to Zero in the Inbox for the first time:**
    - Turn on the Right Side Reading Pane for easy review of emails
    - Move older years out of your Inbox and into Archive folders or move them into new subfolders of the Inbox, named by year or a group of years.
    - Create a folder for the current year and move all but the most recent 3-4 months of emails into it.
    - Review the most recent 3-4 months of emails in your Inbox to look for useful information and tasks.
    - Move valuable information into other systems for reference or action:
        - Move contact information to Contacts
        - Move event or meeting information to the Calendar
        - Save attachments in your electronic document library
        -

- Move emails to email folders if they should remain in your email system
- Print and file what needs to be stored physically
- Add tasks to your Task List

  o Leave Reading in your Inbox and read or delete everything by the end of the week.

- **Use the Right-Click-and-Drag procedure to copy or move an email with a to-do to the Task List** when it holds an action step for you. If you use the *copy* process, be sure to return to the Inbox file the email immediately.

- **To keep your email Inbox low or at zero at all times,** protect time in your day to process email, and alternate these time blocks with those for working on tasks. After creating a number of tasks from emails, be sure to revisit the Task List to reprioritize and make sure your daily task plan is realistic.

Ready to Unleash the Power of YOUR Most Productive Workday?

If you want to increase your productivity and efficiency, reach higher levels of performance and progress, and achieve your goals faster and easier, be sure to visit www.productiveday.com to see the variety of ways you or your team can learn Taskology.

Individual Consulting

Consulting offered by Leslie Shreve is personal, private and powerful. With Leslie personally guiding you, you can learn the entire system of Taskology and dramatically change the way you manage your workload and your workday within four to eight weeks.

Find out more at www.productiveday.com/consulting/.

Team Training

Teamwork is important, but in order for teams and companies to be more productive and get results that impact the bottom line, individual productivity must be mastered FIRST. With Leslie's Taskology for Teams training your team can learn how to work more productively as individuals and work more effectively as a team.

Find out more at www.productiveday.com/team-training/.

Self-Study Programs

You can dramatically increase your productivity and reduce stress by learning Taskology® The Science of Getting Things Done while using the tools you already have. Find out which Taskology product is just right for you and your learning style, whether you choose the binder, the digital download or the video series.

Find out more at http://productiveday.com/products/.

About the Author

Leslie Shreve is the Founder and CEO of Productive Day® and the creator of Taskology® The Science of Getting Things Done, a unique system that teaches simple, logical and easy-to-use strategies to master workload management and significantly increase productivity, progress, and goal achievement for individuals and teams.

For more than 13 years, Leslie worked in corporate office environments before establishing Productive Day in 2003. As a workload management and productivity expert, she has taught hundreds of business leaders and professionals from more than forty different industries how to increase their efficiency and improve their productivity by up to 300% while reducing stress by up to 80%.

Clients previously frustrated or overwhelmed with too much to do, too many emails, and not enough time now claim to have a secret—a new system they can use to take charge of their workday once and for all. Those who learn Taskology are able to gain more clarity, confidence and control in their workday and, as a result, enjoy more time and freedom, focus and progress, and accomplishment and success.

Leslie Shreve
Workload Management and Productivity Expert
Founder and CEO, Productive Day®
Creator of Taskology® The Science of Getting Things Done
www.productiveday.com

Made in the USA
Middletown, DE
22 September 2021